W9-BAB-652

Super freshwater fishing systems

Super freshwater fishing systems

DAVE HARBOUR

STACKPOLE BOOKS

SUPER FRESHWATER FISHING SYSTEMS

Published by
STACKPOLE BOOKS
Cameron and Kelker Streets
Harrisburg, Pa. 17105

ISBN 0-8117-1712-7
Library of Congress Catalog Card Number 76-140748

Printed in U.S.A.

Contents

Foreword

In writing this book the author has sought to accomplish one purpose: to increase materially the reader's probability of catching fish. The author believes that even the oldest fishing pros will be amazed at some of the radical new systems for fooling game fish which this book reveals. And he feels that even the novice angler will have little difficulty understanding these systems and making them pay off.

One individual who looked this material over before publication described the book this way: "The author is consistent; he is bang-bang, special-special, super-super all the way without apology." This reflects the author's attempt to produce the best possible how-to-catch-fish book without any frills or fluff. He strived to waste no words on conventional angling methods already amply covered in other books or on the esthetic concomitants of fishing which any angler will quickly discover for himself. Because of the book's complete preoccupation with tackle and tactics which catch fish, the basic ingredients of all fishing systems, others may call this a "meat fishing" book. That it is! But the author would remind his readers that fish do not have to be killed just because they are caught; they can be released.

The natural curiosity that a good many fishermen have respecting the boats, motors, and so on, owned or personally used by various authors, is rarely gratified. I have no hesitation, however, in branding the bass fishing boat I presently have as the best rig I've ever used. The boat is a Super Skeeter carrying a 35 hp Merc on the stern, and on the bow—a permanently mounted, foot-controlled Motor Guide electric motor. The Vexilar Zonar electronic thermometer has an important and permanent place in my fishing equipment inventory. So does the Lowrance Fish LO-K-TOR, my choice of the electronic, miniaturized Sonar-type fish and depth-finding instruments. Chapter 13 of this book, incidentally, was developed from both my own experience with this equipment and condensation of the booklet *Fun of Electronic Fishing,* published by Lowrance Electronics, 12000 East Skelley Drive, Tulsa, Oklahoma.

This book describes tackle recommended by specific product names. This is to assure instant identification by the reader or his sporting goods clerk and to relieve them of the usual chore of trying to guess what an author means by such vague terms as "a streamlined topwater plug", or "a light wire hook with shank barbs."

Above all else, SUPER FRESHWATER FISHING SYSTEMS is a text for open-minded anglers, novice and expert alike, who truly yearn to increase their angling skills and who are willing to test new and unusual fishing methods fairly. For these anglers, the author earnestly believes this book will provide quick and bountiful dividends.

Dave Harbour

Acknowledgment

Appreciation is expressed to Mr. Ed Murphy, *Sports Afield's* Senior Editor, who inspired the author to undertake the writing of this book; to Capt. Terry Flower and Mr. Carl Lowrance for their direct and valuable assistance in preparation of the manuscript; to critics on the staffs of leading outdoor publications who reviewed and suggested improvements in the manuscript prior to publication; and to friends and fellow anglers across the country who helped develop and test these super fishing systems.

CHAPTER 1

Super Lake-Fishing Systems for Bass

EXPLORING A STRANGE bass lake is one of angling's most exciting adventures. It is the bass fisherman's supreme challenge. The angler who walks away victorious from a bass lake he's never fished before can justly judge himself a bass fisherman. This accomplishment is within the reach of any angler; that is, if he is willing to try a new strategy which works wonders on lake lunkers. This strategy will be summarized under eight general rules.

Rule 1 Make Your Main System The New Super Worm Rig

Since adopting this amazing and unusual worm rig a few years ago, my big bass take has skyrocketed. In the past year, this superior lake fishing rig has given me over fifty largemouths weighing between six and eleven pounds, and from the same lakes where my old conventional tactics never gave me over three or four lunkers a year. It has also skyrocketed my lunker-smallmouth take. This same unusual system has produced similar results for every angler I've coached in its use. I know it can do the same for any reader willing to study seriously the paragraphs which follow.

This lethal system is a method of fishing plastic worms, but it is entirely different from any of the old conventional methods. Several fine distinctions in worm selection, rigging and retrieving are responsible for its lethal effects on lunker bass, largemouths and smallmouths.

The first key distinction in this system for nailing big bass is the use of one very specific type of worm. The worm must be dark purple, very soft, a floater and about six-inches long. A worm like the Creme Wiggle Worm, Series # 100, color No. 36 is recommended. Worms which vary from any of these characteristics will not produce well even when rigged and fished in strict accordance with all other specifications.

For years I labored under the assumption that larger worms would take the biggest bass. This notion has been clearly shot down by many recent tests using worms of various lengths. On all test waters, the six-inch worm outproduced all others by a wide margin. I had always questioned the ability of bass to distinguish between worms of slightly varying shades of color . . .but no longer. In recent months, I have seen too many black, red and light-purple worms whipped by the dark-purple one. Of course, when bass are on a feeding binge, any worm or other

The super worm rig gave the author this ten-pound largemouth.

lure will catch fish, but I have now gathered enough hard evidence to convince me that the soft six-inch purple worm will take them fastest in most situations, and whether the bass are biting well or poorly.

The second key distinction in this unusual worm fishing system is the use of a specific type of hook. The hook must be a short shank # 1 hook with shank barbs and no weed guard. . .a hook like the Eagle Claw Style # 186. When using this rig, a specific type of lively worm motion is required to take lunker bass consistently and this motion cannot be achieved with conventional weedless hooks. The shank barbs are required to hold the worm firmly in the mandatory position on the hook.

The third key distinction in this system is the use of a specific type of hook, leader and swivel arrangement. The #1 hook is attached with a strong knot directly to one end of a fourteen-inch length of pliable leader material and two black snap swivels (# 5's) are snapped together and used to connect the other end of the leader to the line. This hook, leader and swivel arrangement is required to achieve proper worm action and to minimize line twist problems. The swivels also provide that shade of extra weight necessary to just sink the worm and to cast the worm for reasonable distances. Reasonably heavy leader material can be used in this arrangement without significantly diminishing worm action. When fishing for lunker bass, especially in rocky or snag-filled water, a fifteen-pound-test leader is about optimum.

The fourth distinction in this hot bass-producing system is threading the worm on the hook in a very specific manner. The hook point must be carefully inserted in the very center of the worm head; next, the hook must be threaded through the exact center of the worm body until the worm head reaches the eye of the hook; then the hook point must be brought out of the worm body on the flat underside. At this point in threading the worm on the hook, the worm must be pushed slightly further up on the curve of the hook. . .to the exact spot where half the hook curve is exposed; and finally, the head of the worm must be pulled over the eye of the hook and onto the leader.

When the very soft worm is threaded on the hook in this exact manner it will have the proper lively motion when retrieved. . .

but any departure from this technique of putting the worm on the hook will make the worm almost worthless as a bass producer. A related point should also be stressed: after repeated castings or after catching a bass or two, the line often saws through one side of the soft worm head or the hook causes a tear in the worm body. When this happens, the worm will no longer have the required action and should be thrown away. Tougher worms rarely tear, but they don't catch many fish either.

An easy test can reveal whether or not a worm is threaded on the hook properly or whether or not a slightly damaged worm is still effective. When retrieved slowly, a properly threaded and effective worm will wobble in a lively fashion. An improperly threaded or ineffective worm will have little action of any kind.

A shallow and medium-speed retrieve is another interesting distinction in this deadly worm fishing system. The swivel sinks the floating worm very slowly. Instead of those long waits for the worm to sink to the bottom or slowly inching in a heavily-weighted worm, this worm fishing system is much like that faster fishing with plugs or hardware.

Best results with the worm rig are achieved by casting the rig, twitching it a couple of times with rod tip low to sink all line possible, then by retrieving the worm at a medium and even speed. A small percentage of strikes will occur the moment the worm hits the water. Evidence of such strikes is a boil or whirlpool where the worm hits. When this evidence is observed it usually is certain that the bass has the worm and will swallow it if no line pressure is felt. This presents a dilemma. If the swirl indicates the striking bass is a lunker you want to keep, then it should be given slack line for a period of at least half a minute, then the hook should be set with all the might your line will take. If the swirl indicates the striking fish is a yearling you don't wish to keep, then the hook should be set immediately to prevent the fish from swallowing the worm and being hurt by a deep hook.

In the majority of cases, strikes on the super worm rig will occur as the worm is being reeled in with its deadly wiggle at a medium and even speed. A few of these strikes may be vicious and there is no choice but to set the hook immediately and gamble on results. But a far greater number of strikes will be felt

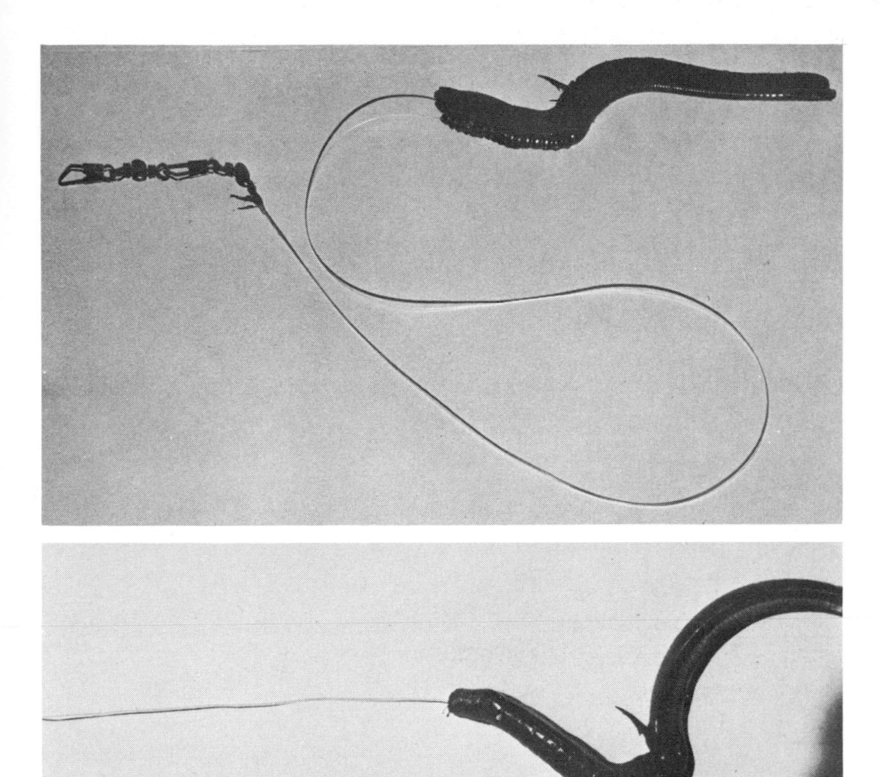

The remarkable super worm rig. Note that worm head is pulled over eye of hook and that worm body bends with hook curve. This precise positioning of worm on hook, plus leader and swivel arrangement shown, cause the worm to "swim-wiggle" like a snake when retrieved through the water. This action can be attained with no other worm rig and it is irresistible to bass.

as very gentle tugs. . .and the most effective way to take these slow "mouthers" is to continue reeling at the same even speed for a few moments as the mouthing continues. . .then to set the hook sharply.

Disciplining oneself to do nothing but what you are already doing when these slow-mouthing strikes occur is the toughest lesson to learn when fishing the new worm rig. The angler's natural inclinations are either to set the hook immediately, or to hit the line release lever and give the fish slack. But either of these reactions will result in losing slow-mouthers. After much practice, however, any angler will learn to feel the gentlest strike during the retrieve, and to "lead" the bass to or around the boat, reeling and maintaining slight line pressure all the while, then setting the hook hard. This results in hooking worm-munchers instead of losing them.

Practice will also teach the angler to distinguish between most lunkers and yearlings which are slowly munching the worm during the retrieve. A mouthing lunker feels almost like a slow-moving log or a dragging weed or piece of moss. . .while the mouthing yearling imparts subtle but sharp gentle twitches to the rod tip. If you judge the muncher to be a lunker, lead him at least half a minute before setting the hook. . .but if you judge him to be a yearling, set the hook immediately.

The use of any plastic worm rig, even when one uses the precautions just discussed, will result in some bass being hurt too badly to release. So if you want to release every bass you catch, use other lures. On the other hand, by using the precautions just discussed, it is possible to fish worms and hurt only a very small percentage of fish. To those of us who love bass, this is perhaps, the most important of all skills one can develop.

A sharp two-man fishing system often will further increase lunker catches. This involves the lead man in the boat using a topwater plug and the second using the worm rig. Many bass which make a pass at the plug, but are not hooked, will take the worm a few seconds later. The topwater plug probably excites many bass too cautious to actually hit the plug, puts them in the mood for striking, and causes a larger percentage to then take the worm.

Although this system usually will outfish other bass fishing methods in most lakes, it's not the solution to all the bass fisherman's problems. Occasionally, other lures will outfish this worm rig. And this system, like any other, is likely to produce well only when it is augmented by skillful and persistent casting concentrated in promising bass waters, a subject to be discussed shortly.

The recommended worm and swivel terminal gear is on the light side for easy casting with the average casting outfit. This problem can be licked by using six or eight pound test lines on long, light and fast-tip-action spinning, spincasting or casting rods. However, most bass water has generous amounts of grass, lilies or snags which most lunker bass will head directly for when hooked; therefore, using those easy-to-cast-with light lines is rarely practical if the angler is interested in landing the real lunkers. A fifteen pound test line will give the angler reasonable probability of landing the lunkers, and with a little practice most anglers can throw the light worm rig far enough with such lines, especially if they use a spinning or spincasting reel with a long fast-tip-action rod. "Far enough" is on the order of twenty to thirty feet.

Most of the time, big bass are lazy and one must drop the worm on top of them to make them strike. Therefore, dotting likely cover edges with short casts is far more productive than hitting them at widely-spaced intervals with fewer long casts. Of course, if you are casting a bank from thirty feet out, it is important to ease the boat along quietly and to stay seated while casting in order not to spook your quarry, especially if the water is clear and calm.

Going over to this new worm fishing system will change many of any angler's old concepts about bass fishing, if he'll give it a fair test. For example, most anglers labor under the assumption that the highest probability of catching big bass in the hot summer months is enjoyed by those with enough gumption to fish deep lake water. If the angler uses the new worm rig properly he will discover that the opposite is often true.

Summer water temperatures are usually constant at any depth in lakes of the Far South, and there this system will take strings of hot-weather lunkers consistently from the shallows where bass most often feed . . . and it will do so almost as often in the middle of the day as during the early or late hours.

In those deep lakes further north, summer temperatures are cooler in deep water, and bass spend most of their time there except when they go on feeding binges. Since feeding bass are often shallow, this shallow worm rig pays off often in summer in these lakes, too. This rig is deadly in the cool spring and fall months in any lake anywhere. In the Deep South it works all winter.

When bass stay deep, as they occasionally do for long periods, the super worm rig, with one simple modification, can still be deadly. Just add a 1/16th or 1/8th slip sinker on the line above the swivels. This sinks the worm fast and keeps it deep on a slow retrieve. When a bass in the depths is felt mouthing the lure, the angler should keep leading him for a few moments before setting the hook. Then set the hook hard. When dragging deep snag-filled bottoms, it may be necessary to make the super rig weedless. This can be done by hooking the worm through only about 1/4 inch of the worm head, then by pulling the head over the hook eye onto the line, then by sinking the hook point and barb just into the worm body.

Hooking the worm on the hook in this manner will not enable the worm to achieve the maximum amount of lively action, but it will produce far more bass in deep snag-filled water than will most worms fished on the old weedless hooks or jig heads.

Rule 2 Fish Hard . . . All Day Long . . . Fair Weather Or Foul

Prospecting for bass, especially in a strange lake, is similar to any form of prospecting. A long hard search is usually required to find the treasure. In comparison, digging it out is easy. Therefore, the angler's chances for finding bass also are influenced largely by the amount of hard, steady, persistent fishing time he's willing and able to expend.

Most modern bass specialists start off with the sound premise that it is not possible to predict when or where bass will feed in any lake they do not know. The fact that most big bass feed in loose schools or packs is still contested by some anglers of the old school who have not been successful in establishing this fact for themselves. Nevertheless, it is true.

Most modern bass masters know full well that they'll likely take most of their bass from a strange lake from one or two general areas and during one or two short periods rarely lasting more than an hour. It is no longer a secret to them that bass of respectable size most often feed in loose schools and make one or two short but all-out feeding excursions daily. The fact that these big bass feeding excursions may take place in the very middle of hot summer days, and even in very hot and shallow water, also is widely accepted by most knowledgeable anglers today. So is the fact that "jackpot" feeding periods probably will take place whether the weather is fair, foul or in-between. For these reasons,

Lunker bass action is rarely generated by accident. It most often results from careful lure selection, concentrated fishing efforts in big-bass water, and hard persistent fishing. (Photo by Tom Dewberry)

the pro who wins tournaments consistently fishes each lake without let-up. Only the same brand of persistent all-day, all-weather angling is likely to reward the occasional angler with a jackpot bass interception.

Fishing without let-up also means not wasting fishing time. The use of a slow, under-powered boat means piddling away valuable fishing time while reconnoitering big lake shorelines and while moving from one fishing area to another. And the use of any boat not equipped with an electric motor means wasting valuable fishing time paddling or sculling. So, if you're renting a bass boat for a strange-lake expedition, it will pay to rent one equipped with a reasonably powerful outboard and with an electric motor—foot-propelled, if possible. If you're thinking of buying a bass boat, new or used, take a tip from the pros and consider carefully the advantages of having a maneuverable streamlined boat with efficient, time-saving power packages at both ends. I use a boat with a conventional outboard on the stern and a foot-controlled electric motor permanently mounted on the bow. All controls for both motors are within easy reach of my swivel-chair pilot seat in the bow. I can move at nearly 40mph across a lake, traverse water only a few inches deep, and never have to waste casting time by picking up an oar or walking to the rear to start a motor. Of all bass fishing boats I have used, this is my favorite. Of course, the use of large motors is not permitted on some lakes, and only canoes, kayaks or car-top boats can be launched in others.

Rule 3 Work Good Bass Cover Near Deep Water

In most big lakes, schools of big bass, as well as solitary lunkers, spend most of their time in deep water close to feeding areas. When the urge strikes, the fish ease en masse to the feeding areas, spread out in the cover and begin gorging. Feeding areas are nearly always those with good bait-fish-harboring cover, such

Foot-controlled electric motors are ideal for bass fishing. They relieve the angler of paddling duties, leaving both hands free for casting.

as weed, lily or hyacinth patches, brush or stumps, rocky ledges or rock piles.

Because of these factors, all available fishing time should be concentrated in areas where such cover is abundant and close to deep water. No other single tactic is more important when exploring a strange lake for big bass. Measuring water depth as you fish is easy when using a good fish locator. And the locator also enables the angler to spot good underwater bass cover, such as brush or rock piles.

Concentrated angling effort near good cover close to deep water is a big key to locating lunker bass.

Yes, concentrating angling efforts along banks close to good cover near deep water provides the angler his best chance of hitting a school of big bass during a feeding period. And this tactic also provides him the best chance of picking up a careless lunker during other periods. Hooking a single lunker may be a tip-off on an area where a bass school will feed sometime during the day. Therefore, it is wise practice to mark well each area where even a stray bass of respectable size is hooked, and to recheck these areas for other feeding fish each couple of hours during the day.

Rule 4 Start Out With Artificials

Exploring the vast shoreline of a big lake is a monumental task even when the angler confines his angling efforts to areas of most promising cover. Therefore, the highest probability of locating bass in a strange lake is enjoyed by the angler who can test-fish the most good water per hour. Heaving artificials with a good casting stick and giving top priority to the super worm rig just described, gives the angler this important advantage. Far more water can be fished, horizontally and vertically, in any given period of time by heaving lures with a long-range casting, spin-casting or spinning outfit than can be fished by using either a flyrod or bait. Fly fisherman and bait addicts can still have their fun after the bass are located.

While test-fishing a stretch of water near good bass cover, it is usually best to ease along at a medium-low speed, rather than at the very slow speed which pays off for casting after bass concentrations are located. The "fast" switch position on most electric motors eases most boats along at about the desired speed for exploratory casting. It is also good practice to move downwind when test-fishing bass water, for this improves both boat control and casting ease and accuracy. Test-fishing casts need not be long to be effective; but they must be accurate. In most waters, especially in the summer, feeding bass will be lying in cover or at cover edges and will rarely move more than a couple of feet to take a lure. Therefore, any cast which falls more than a foot or so from cover is usually a wasted cast.

Rule 5 Pound The Points And Coves

As previously indicated, if a bass school is on a feeding binge, the fish will usually be spread out along a stretch of cover; most often one at least twenty yards long. It is for this reason that moving along and test-fishing at the "fast" electric motor speed was recommended. Spot casting good cover at about ten-yard intervals is ample for locating a feeding bass school. As further insurance for not missing a concentration of bass on a feeding binge, be sure to pound each good point and cove.

In the South, the best bass cover is often a long fringe of grass or tree line growing in the water, sometimes well out from the bank. If bass are feeding in the area, a good bass will almost always be occupying each point and each small cove formed by the grass fringe or tree line.

In the Central and Western States, the best bass cover is often a rocky ledge. Again, if bass are feeding along the ledge, it is almost certain that a good bass will occupy each point and each cove formed by the ledge. The same is true when fishing any form of cover. So, when test-fishing cover edges, always try to hit each good point and each good cove. Pay less attention to straight lines of coves, for they may or may not harbor bass, even if a school is feeding in the area.

Rule 6 Watch For Feeding Bass

Test-fishing stretches of good bass cover often is the only dependable method for locating bass in a strange lake. However, feeding bass will sometimes create signs on the water surface which the watchful angler also can detect and capitalize on. These signs of feeding bass are occasionally obvious; such as, water being churned by one or more big minnow-chasers. And no angler will miss such obvious signs of bass on feeding binges. Far more often, however, the signs of feeding bass are subtle and difficult to detect, especially during the hot months. Getting into the habit of watching for and reading these more common and subtle signs can pay big dividends when exploring a strange lake.

Three subtle signs most often reveal the position of feeding bass to the discerning angler: (1) slight dimples or boils on the water surface; (2) the vibration of reeds, weeds, or twigs protruding from the water; and (3) erratic movement of bait fish on the surface. Slight dimples or boils on the surface are made by bass striking at bait fish below the surface where big bass most often feed. The twitching of reeds, weeds or branches protruding from the water often is caused by bass "butting" around in cover to drive out minnows, crayfish or shrimp. And bait fish darting erratically along the surface often are maneuvering to escape from bass feeding below. When any of these subtle signs are observed, the immediate area around it should be thoroughly fished.

Rule 7 When A Feeding Bass Area Is Located, Pound The Area With Artificials Or Bait

When feeding bass are located by test-fishing or by observing signs of their presence, the angler should pound that area thoroughly, but cautiously so he doesn't spook the fish. A concentration of big bass is likely to feed for only a short period. This is the golden opportunity for stringer-filling, and for a shot at a real trophy. It is the opportunity that all the preceding hard work and test-fishing was designed to bring about. It is the one opportunity no angler should fail to exploit.

To exploit the interception of a feeding bass school, the angler should immediately design a sound casting plan. This plan should recognize that many or at least several bass are probably feeding in the area (usually along a cover line) where the first bass was hooked or where feeding fish were sighted. It should also recognize that maneuvering the boat too close to the feeding area, or standing up while casting, is likely to spook the fish and blow the whole big moment.

Because of the above factors, the best initial tactic is to ease the boat out from the feeding cover and to circle back behind the spot where the first bass was hooked or sighted. If using an electric motor, the switch should be placed on the "slow" position and the angler should begin pinpointing the cover edges with careful casts. Casts should be made to every foot of cover edge until the point is again reached where the first fish was hooked or sighted. The same careful and thorough kind of cover-edge casting should be continued well beyond the point of first contact.

At all times the boat should be well out from the bank. Each time a bass is hooked, the boat should be headed out to deep water to keep the fighting fish out of cover. This not only increases the angler's chances for landing each lunker, but it also decreases the probability of spooking the whole bass school by having to maneuver the boat into cover to unsnag a fish. Each time a fish is maneuvered out from bank and landed, the boat should again be circled back to the point where the fish was hooked and thorough cover-edge casting should be resumed.

When an area is reached where casts no longer produce a strike, the angler should make a circle well out from bank and back to the farthest point of contact. Then he should re-work the entire stretch of fish-producing cover. When this strategy ceases to produce strikes, the angler should resume his search for another feeding bass school. But first, he should make a careful mental note of the location of the feeding area for use in case he fishes the lake another time.

When working a feeding area, it is usually best to stick to the lure which produced the initial strike, at least during the first "pass" through the area. The super worm rig, just described, is a top test-fishing choice. If that lure fails to produce well during the first pass, and in cases where the angler is working an area where he has only observed bass feeding, it is wise to make several passes through the probable feeding area using different lures. If a bass concentration is actually feeding in the area, this tactic is apt to reveal the lure the fish want in short order.

Occasionally, bass may be spotted feeding far back in thick cover, such as grass or lily pads. In this situation, a large, streamlined, and very weedless lure is usually the best choice. The Lake Jackson Special, a big 8″ jointed weedless worm, works wonders in weeds and grass. This big worm with its fast-swinging flip tail rides the surface and stirs up plenty of action as it is pulled through the thick cover. It is weedless with a capital "W" and climbs cleanly over or through the thickest weeds or grass without fouling. Other good lures for extracting bass from the thick stuff include the Shimmy Wiggler, Tarantula, and Silver Minnow, all fished with pork rind and retrieved fast, on top of the water.

Live bait can also be deadly when a concentration of feeding bass is located. Large shiners, or other large minnows native to the water being fished, usually are the hottest offerings for the real lunkers. The most effective tactic for fishing live bait is to anchor the boat well out from the feeding area and to spot-cast cover fringes. A rig without weight and a small cork is usually best for this type fishing. Since long periods of test-fishing with artificials is usually required to locate a feeding bass school in the first place, the angler must be equipped properly in order to keep minnows alive. A screen-type minnow bucket can be dragged along in the water at electric motor speeds. However, the most practical minnow bucket for a strange-lake exploration trip is one also equipped with a battery-operated aerator.

Rule 8 Carry Along An Adequate Lure Supply

Although the super worm rig is most likely to be the hottest bass producer in any lake, it is wise to carry along a reasonable supply of other good lures, too. The following categories will constitute an adequate arsenal for any bass lake:

a. 6″ purple, soft plastic worms rigged for shallow and deep fishing as previously recommended. Examples: Creme Wiggle Worms, Bass Buster Worms, Fliptail Worms, Hardhead Worms.

b. 8″ black or purple weedless worms for fishing on top in very heavy grass or lilies. Example: C & H Lake Jackson Special.

c. Floating thin minnow-imitation plugs in silver or gold colors (for top and shallow water fishing). Examples: Finlandia, Rapala, Rebel, Cobra, Bang-O-Lure, Hellcat. These lures often pay off when bass are gorging on minnows at or near the surface.

d. Sinking thin minnow-imitation plugs in silver or gold finish (for medium-depth fishing). Examples: Weighted Finlandia and Rebel, Countdown Rapala. These lures are excellent for medium-depth trolling and for fishing rocky edges of western impoundments.

e. Top-water popping plugs in natural and frog finish. Examples: Pico Flasher, Jitterbug, Dalton Special, Lucky 13, Torpedo. These fun-to-fish-with lures often pay off in the shallows, especially during the spring and fall.

f. Big-lip, bottom-bouncing, wobbling plugs in silver or natural finish for deep fishing. Examples: Hellbender, Bomber, Stingray. These are often the hottest of all lures for deep-water trolling.

g. Weedless spoons and spinners rigged with pork rind or pork frog. Examples: Tarantula, Spider, Silver Minnow, Sprite, Shimmy Wiggler. These are often top producers when bass are in thick weeds, pads or murky water.

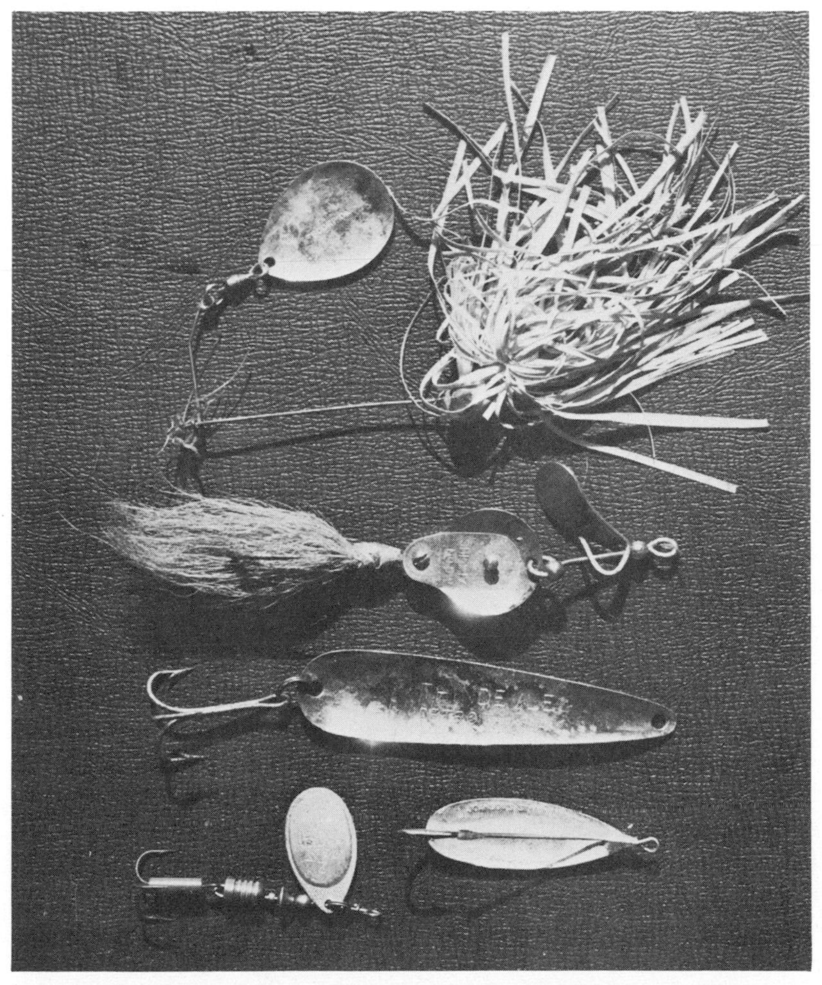

Examples of good bass hardware: ***Top to bottom*****—Ward Spider; Shimmy Wiggler; Thin Devle; Mepps Spinner and Silver Minnow.**

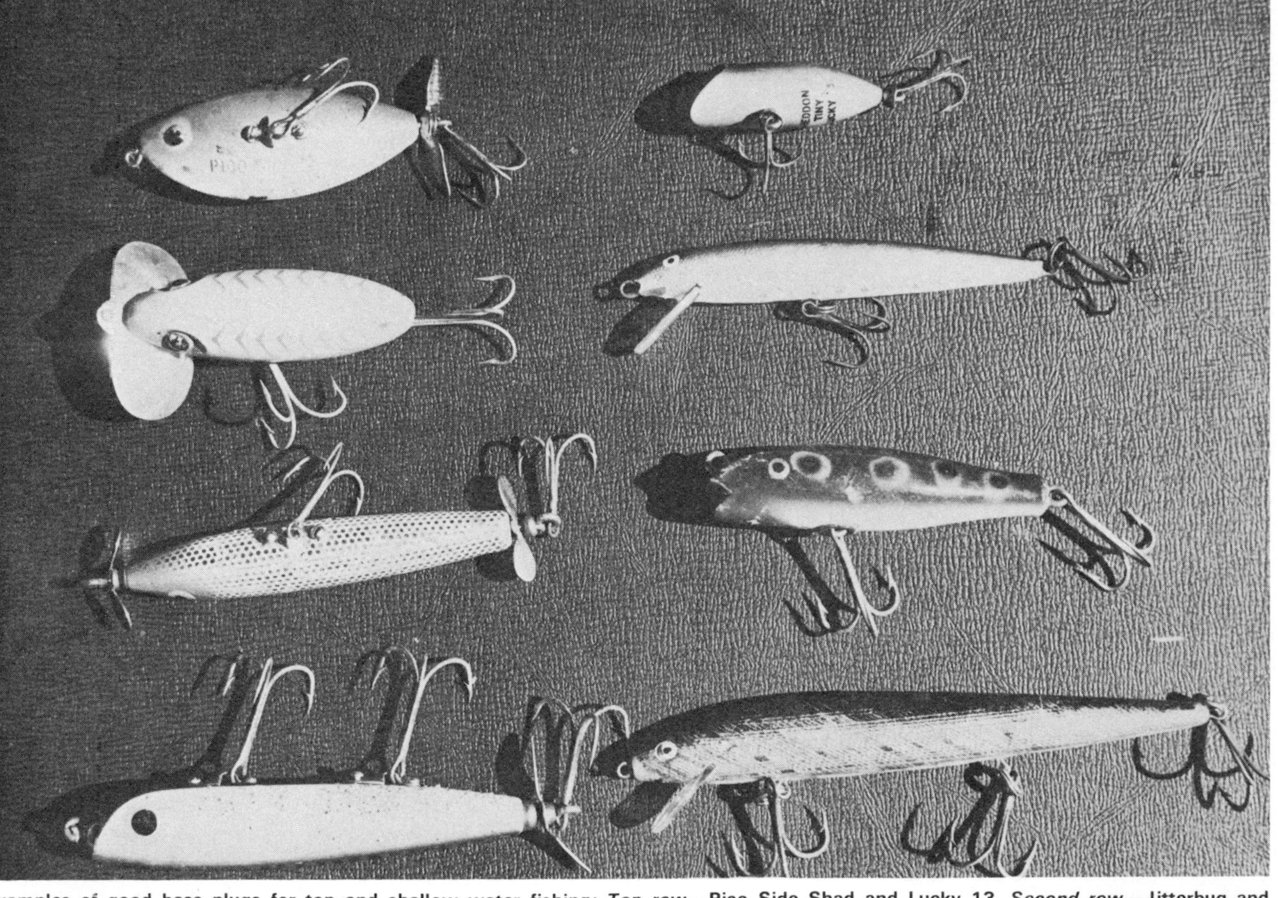

Examples of good bass plugs for top and shallow water fishing: *Top row*—Pico Side Shad and Lucky 13. *Second row*—Jitterbug and

CHAPTER 2

Super Stream-Fishing Systems for Bass

LARGEMOUTHS OR smallmouths thrive in nearly every type of stream in the country including small streams and large streams, warm streams and comparatively cold streams, brushy streams and open streams, inland streams and salty coastal streams, streams winding through swamps and those creeping across deserts, fast-moving streams and slow-moving streams, and even non-running streams with only occasional holes containing water. Yet, most bass anglers stick to lake fishing and thousands of the nation's top bass-loaded streams are under-fished. This chapter is designed to give busy anglers a complete but thumbnail sketch of the real pay-off methods for fishing our many different kinds of bass streams with plugs, hardware, flies, or bait.

How To Choose A Good Bass Stream

The first basic problem the serious bass angler interested in stream fishing must work is identifying those particular streams in his area which contain the highest concentration of bass, for successful bass fishing hinges largely upon confining angling efforts to precisely such streams. This is no easy problem to solve, since any of the many kinds of streams just described may or may not contain sizable populations of bass. A little logical thought and research, however, can narrow down that list of streams in any area which are most likely to be the top bass producers. The most likely bass-producing streams in any area are those which warrant a "Yes" answer to all of the following questions:

a. Is the stream normally clear? A stream which is normally clear or only slightly roily usually supports a larger bass population than does a normally muddy stream; and bass action is usually much faster in clear water because the fish can see lures and baits at greater ranges.

b. Does the stream have deep holes? Streams with at least occasional deep holes are always the best bass fishing choices for few bass, especially lunkers, will hold in any stream without the protection afforded by pockets of deep water. This does not mean that the stream must be large. Small easily-wadable streams with only scattered holes five to ten feet deep are often top bass producers.

c. Is the stream free of pollution? Heavy pollution, of course, can make the best potential bass stream barren or nearly so. This point is especially important for urban anglers to keep in mind. For example, the Potomac River above Washington, D. C. is a good largemouth and smallmouth stream; but below the Capitol city there is practically no bass fishing because of pollution. This same pattern holds on many streams in the vicinity of cities.

d. Does the temperature of the stream range between 65 degrees and 75 degrees? Largemouths and spotted bass prefer water temperatures of 68 degrees to 75 degrees and smallmouths prefer water temperatures of 65 degrees to 70 degrees; therefore, streams with these water temperatures usually contain the highest concentrations of bass, and stream bass usually strike best when water temperatures are within these ranges. However, northern and western bass will sometimes strike when water temperatures hover around the 60 degrees mark, and bass in the

Small easily-wadable streams with only scattered holes five to ten feet deep are often top bass producers. (Courtesy, Florida News Bureau)

Deep South often will strike when water temperatures soar to 85 degrees or even 90 degrees.

Yes, the "best bet" bass streams in any area are those which warrant a "Yes" answer to all four basic questions just outlined. All streams which pass this basic test are likely to harbor respectable concentrations of active bass. However, the cream of these "best bet" bass streams are likely to be those which pass still another test: Is the stream lightly fished? Of course, no large bass stream and few small bass streams are ever "fished out;" however, bass in a lightly fished stream are far easier to tease into striking than are bass in a heavily fished stream. This is probably because bass in a heavily fished stream become lure and bait shy . . . but the reason is not important. The important point is that this fact is true. Therefore, concentrating angling efforts in lightly fished streams provides additional insurance for catching more bass and bigger bass.

Bass streams most likely to be lightly fished are often found in what appear to be very unlikely locations. Small, unproductive-looking streams, often in the shadows of busy cities, probably constitute the largest single category of top bass streams which are lightly fished. Any small stream meeting the criteria for good bass fishing already discussed may be one of the hottest and most neglected bass producers in any area. This is especially true of any small stream which feeds into a larger stream or lake containing bass, for bass migrate up such small streams during high water periods and often remain in the deeper pools when the water goes down. Tagged bass have been recovered indicating migration of more than ten miles up such streams. Especially in mid-summer and fall, many of these small streams contain only widely-spaced holes of water and these holes are often crammed with stranded and starved bass which will gobble up almost any lure or bait thrown at them. Often these choice bass holes cannot be seen from highway bridges which cross the stream. Consequently, anglers often rush by this red-hot bass fishing in their own backyards heading for distant, but mediocre bass waters.

For years, I enjoyed fantastic fishing for both largemouths and smallmouths in small streams within a short drive of the crowded Washington, D. C. area and seldom saw other fishermen. These small-size, big-bass producers included Goose Creek, Broad Run, Bull Run, Passage Creek and headwaters of the North and South Forks of the Shenandoah River. In all sections of the country I've located similar streams in heavily-populated areas: small, unproductive-looking streams, but streams with plenty of big, hungry bass and little angling pressure.

A second category of highly productive and lightly fished bass streams are those countless small brackish-water streams which enter bays and bayous all along the southern half of the East Coast and along the entire Gulf Coast. Many of these streams are accessible only by boat; however, many others are crossed by roads and can be easily reached, then waded or fished from the bank. These coastal streams are probably neglected by most bass fishermen because they simply don't realize that buster bass thrive in brackish water. Brackish-water largemouths grow big and sassy on brackish-water minnows and crabs, and these particularly active bass abound in quantity in nearly all southeastern and southern coastal streams. The angler who takes the time to locate and fish such streams is not only likely to hit a black bass jackpot but he may also string weakfish, channel bass, flounder and snook in some coastal streams at the same time.

Other top bass fishing streams where fishing pressure is usually light are those which are simply hard to get to or difficult to fish. These include inland streams, large and small, which are too deep to wade and with banks too brushy to walk along or cast from, and those well hidden streams which meander through tangles of swampy jungle.

Best Times To Fish A Bass Stream

Any time the angler can go fishing is a good time to fish a bass stream in spring, summer, or fall, and in the winter in the Deep South. This is because stream bass are far less finicky about striking than are lake bass. There are certain periods, however, when stream bass usually feed with increased gusto, and therefore strike lures and take bait best. These "best bet" fishing periods are:

a. Late afternoons following warm, sunshiny days during winter and cold spring and fall months.

b. Nights, early mornings and misty and cloudy periods during hot summer, spring and fall months.

c. Whenever the stream is on a slight rise, but is not muddy.

d. During rising tide periods on coastal streams affected by tides.

Best Lures And Baits For Stream Bass

As a general rule, in the very cold winter months and in the very hot summer months, largemouths and smallmouths in a large and very deep and slow-moving stream can be most easily taken on deep running lures and baits fished on or near the bottom. In all other stream fishing situations, almost any category of lures or baits will take stream bass almost any season of the year.

This is because, unlike lakes, most streams have enough current to keep water temperatures almost constant at all levels, and because bass suspended anywhere in most streams can see a lure or bait passing near them at any level, from top to bottom.

Forty years of bass chasing convinces me that any angler who heads for a bass stream with a couple of lures or baits in each of the following categories will be well armed for largemouths, smallmouths or spotted bass:

Category 1: Medium-size top-water bass plugs in natural fish or frog colors, lures such as Dalton Special, Crippled Minnow, Lucky 13, Jitterbug, Finlandia, Rapala, Rebel, Viper, Cobra, Hellcat.

Category 2: Medium-size spinner-type or spoon-type lures in silver, gold or black colors and fished with short strips of white or black pork rind; lures such as Mepps, Abu-Reflex, Scorpion, Hawaiian Wiggler, Panther Martin, Rooster Tail, Dardevle, Sprite or Silver Minnow.

Category 3: Plastic worms in purple, or long thin chunks of black pork rind (usually the best of all stream lures for lunker bass).

Category 4: (for the flyfisherman) Large streamers, floating feathered minnows, rubber grasshoppers.

Category 5: (for the bait fisherman) Minnows native to the stream being fished, salamanders, crayfish, frogs, hellgrammites.

Shaping Up For Stream Casting

The angler who chooses a good bass stream in accordance with the criteria previously outlined, who heads for that stream during a favorable fishing period and who totes along a few lures or baits in the categories just recommended, will be well on his way to filling his stringer; that is, if he can cast a stream effectively. Stream casting with flyrod or with casting, spincasting or spinning equipment is far more difficult than casting a lake. In most stream fishing situations, the lure must be placed in a small preselected area on each cast, and in most cases the lure also must be propelled to that point through small openings in the brush or under overhanging tree limbs. This means that the successful stream angler must sharpen up his casting eye and arm to the point where he can vary and maintain constant control of the trajectory of his lure from the moment it leaves his rod until it drops at the preselected point.

Most anglers with any casting experience can drop their lure reasonably close to where they want it, but few are proficient enough to get the lure there through small openings in brush or under tree branches as they must do to cast most streams effectively. Unless the angler learns to vary and maintain constant control of the trajectory of his lure, he might as well confine his fishing to open lakes, for if he heads for the typical bass stream, he'll spend most of his time trying to extract lures from trees and brush.

A few afternoons each week devoted to practice-casting in the backyard is the easiest way to learn to vary and control lure trajectory. The hardware caster should stick with his favorite long-range casting outfit. Any of them will work fine on the brushy stream. The flyfisherman should use a short rod, a heavy line and a short leader. Use practice casting plugs or flies without hooks. Any reasonably small object, such as a bucket or an old tire, will serve as a suitable target. String a rope up between your casting position and that of the target. Learn to hit the target by casting under the rope. Vary the height of the rope above the ground and its position between you and the target. Then stand a couple of long sticks up against the rope five or six feet apart to simulate openings in the brush. Learn to hit the target by casting between the sticks, both below and above the rope. Practice-casting like this can make any angler proficient at varying and controlling the trajectory of his lure in a short time. Then he'll be ready to take on stream bass anywhere.

How To Read A Bass Stream

Bass are likely to hold only in restricted areas in any stream. The angler who learns how to glance at a stream and determine where these likely bass lairs are has taken another big step toward filling his stringer with good fish, for he won't be wasting his time fishing long stretches of unproductive water. As previously indicated, only streams with at least occasional deep holes are likely to contain many bass to begin with; and in any stream, large or small, most of the bass, especially lunkers, will be congregated in these deep holes, or in shallow water nearby. Long stretches of shallow water between deep holes are usually barren of bass and are a waste of time to fish.

Bass, especially lunkers, like to hole up in the shade as well as in deep water; therefore, shady areas in deep holes are likely lunker lairs. Shadowy water against steep banks, tree stumps or trunks, or under thick overhanging bushes or under floating or submerged logs, are top spots in a deep pool to nail granddaddy bass. In fast streams, smallmouths also tend to congregate in the headwaters of deep pools, while largemouths and spotted bass usually prefer the quieter mid-pool waters. However, when stream bass go on feeding binges, they sometimes make excursions into the shallows both above and below deep pools. Lunker bass, however, will rarely be found more than fifty yards from the safety of deep water.

The very best bass holes on any stream are usually those which lie just below high dams or waterfalls the fish cannot leap. Other particularly productive bass fishing holes are: (1) those deep

Bass, especially lunkers, like to hole up in the shade as well as in or near deep water. So, the stream angler after big bass should concentrate his angling efforts in precisely such spots. (Courtesy, Florida Development Comm.)

holes on brackish water streams which lie immediately above open bays and bayous; and (2) those deep holes on any stream which lie immediately above the confluence of that stream with a deep lake or larger stream containing bass.

How To Approach A Good Bass Hole

Whether the angler is using bait, flies or casting hardware, he must get his offering to his quarry without being seen or "heard," for a spooked bass is highly unlikely to take any bait or lure. Two basic but all-important precautions can enable the angler to approach within easy casting range of stream bass.

First, the angler should approach from downstream. If there's any current, bass will be lying with their heads pointing upstream and they can't see nearly as far downstream as upstream. And bass "hear" by feeling vibrations carried through the water. These vibrations, such as the noise made by a motor or by a wading angler sloshing through the water, travel a long distance with the current, but only a short distance against it.

Second, the angler should approach each good bass hole in a crouched position if wading, and in a sitting position if in a boat. The higher the profile of the angler above the water, the further he can be seen by bass. It's little trouble to bend down while wading up to a good bass pool, and it's not good practice to stand up in a boat any time. Approaching a good bass hole from the shady side of the stream and staying in fairly deep water if wading, provides further insurance for closing on bass without spooking them. If the angler observes these simple precautions when approaching each good bass hole, he will be able to get close enough to his quarry undetected to keep his casts short and accurate, the kind of casts which always take stream bass fastest.

Wade-Fishing And Float-Fishing Equipment

Many small bass streams can be fished comfortably and effectively during the hot months without waders or float equipment. Only a pair of tennis shoes or sneakers to protect the feet, jeans or duck trousers to protect the legs from thorns or briars and a long-sleeved shirt to reduce exposure to insect bites and poison ivy are needed. Of course, during the cooler months, chest-high waders and warm trousers and socks and warm jacket are desirable for wading any bass stream.

The floating innertube with canvas seat, and shoulder straps which hold the innertube in place while the angler is wading, is a tremendous aid when fishing many bass streams. This rig makes a true amphibian out of the angler. It enables him to fish stretches of stream too deep to wade without having to climb up and over steep and brushy banks. It enables him to fish deep stretches of streams which boats cannot get to because of dangerous rapids or shallow rocky water up or downstream. When using this rig, the angler can wade and continue casting with both hands free when he comes to shallow water, and he can continue casting from his comfortable seat when he comes to deep water. This rig even protects the angler from unpleasant dunkings when he slips on slippery rocks while wading shallow water for, when he does lose his footing, he merely drops down into his comfortable canvas seat. Of course, during cool weather, a good pair of chest-high waders is required when using the innertube rig to keep the angler dry and warm. A canvas creel or vest with pockets for carrying lures, bait or flies, and a stringer, complete the special equipment needed for fishing a stream wth innertube.

A boat, of course, is the only practical platform to use when fishing many large bass streams. The kind of boat which should be used depends upon the kind of stream being fished. As a general rule, the boat should always be large enough and equipped with sufficient power to be safe in the kind of water being fished, yet be small enough to provide reasonable control and maneuverability for casting.

As previously stressed, when possible, the boat should be maneuvered upstream and casts should be made upstream. In streams with very slow current, small boats and small motors are ideal platforms for upstream bass fishing. However, in big streams with fast currents, larger boats and larger motors are required for safety and to ease the boat upstream against the heavy current.

Of course, some bass can be caught while floating downstream in an innertube or in rubber rafts, canoes, or small, low-draft and light aluminum or plastic boats. Most successful downstream floaters, however, float on below the best bass holes, let the holes "rest" for ten or fifteen minutes, then approach these choice holes from downstream as previously recommended.

Best System For Casting The Bass Stream

Yes, sharpening up the eye and arm for stream casting, knowing how to choose a good bass stream, knowing how to identify the best holes and the most likely lunker lairs in or near those holes, knowing the importance of the stealthy, upstream approach, and being properly equipped with wade or float-fishing gear and with a few good lures or baits . . . these are the basic ingredients of a successful bass fishing trip to any stream. However, expert casting tactics are also essential.

Good bass holes should be fished thoroughly. As the angler approaches each good bass hole, he should make a few casts in the shallows below the hole, then make repeated casts in the deep hole itself. Every good hole on most bass streams contains a few lunker bass, and these lunkers must sometimes be "teased" into striking by repeatedly passing a lure or bait by them. After thoroughly casting the deep hole, a few casts should then be made in the shallows just above the hole; then the angler should waste no time proceeding to the next good hole. The more good holes the angler can cast thoroughly in a given period of time the higher his chances are for accumulating a good string of big bass.

Lures and baits should be dropped close to banks or other cover. The point has already been made that most likely lunker lairs in the good bass holes are in dark shadowy water against steep banks, trunks or stumps . . . or under floating or submerged cover, such as logs or brush. A lure or bait which is dropped within a few inches of such cover is far more likely to produce a strike than one which falls a few feet from it. This is precisely the reason so much emphasis was placed earlier on the importance of learning to cast accurately before heading for a bass stream.

Tips On Casting Topwater Plugs

Topwater plugs should be allowed to float downstream with the current and "twitched" occasionally. Bass will usually charge a

Big topwater plugs, such as the Dalton Special, are excellent smallmouth lures. They should be allowed to float downstream with the current and "twitched" occasionally for best results.

topwater plug floating downstream at current speed much more readily than one retrieved against the current or downstream faster than the current. This is equally true of smallmouths in fast-moving water or largemouths or spotted bass in slow-moving water. However, the floating plug should be given an occasional "pop" or "twitch" to make it appear lifelike. It's very difficult to set the hook when a bass strikes a topwater plug floating with the current. Therefore, the angler should also keep all slack line reeled in and set the hook hard the instant the strike occurs. When fishing a hole with no current, the topwater plug should be fished still on the water for long periods between "pops" or "twitches."

Tips On Casting Spinners And Spoons

Spinners and spoons should be retrieved downstream just faster than the current. Most bass will not charge a spinner or spoon cranked furiously downstream any faster than they will strike a lure cranked in against the current. For maximum results, the rule is: keep the spinner or spoon moving just fast enough to impart action to the lure.

This means the spinner or spoon should always be reeled downstream just a bit faster than the current. This, of course, requires fast reeling if the current is fast, and slow reeling if the current is slow. In a stream with no current, the very slow retrieve is usually best. And to fool lunker bass, don't forget to hang that short strip of pork rind on all spinners and spoons as previously recommended.

Tips On Casting Plastic Worms And Pork Rind Chunks

Plastic worms and pork rind chunks should be fished with as little weight as possible and allowed to drift downstream naturally with the current.

There is no better all-around lure than the purple worm or black pork rind chunk for lunker stream bass—if fished correctly. However, these lures are far harder to fish correctly in most streams, especially those with fast currents, than they are in still lakes. The first trick is to stay away from those heavy jig heads which many lake anglers use in fishing these lures. Instead, plastic worms should be rigged and fished on the hot new hook-and-swivel rig as recommended in the preceding chapter. Pork rind chunks should be hooked through the hole in the front section.

Both the plastic worm and the pork rind chunk should be occasionally twitched as they are allowed to drift naturally downstream. The moment the strike in a stream is felt, the angler should be prepared to strip out line so that the bass feels no line resistance. The bass should be allowed to run with the bait for about ten seconds before the hook is set. This usually will assure the hook being well within the mouth of the bass, so that it can be driven home.

Tips On Fly Casting

Those large streamers, floating feathered minnows and rubber grasshoppers previously recommended for stream bass also should be allowed to float downstream naturally with the current.

It is almost impossible to flycast effectively with these comparatively heavy offerings on the typical brushy stream unless that short rod, heavy line and short leader previously recommended are used. The leader need not exceed four feet in length and should be kept to about six-pounds test for this type of fishing. The same accurate and repeated casting in deep holes and near good bass cover as recommended for the hardware tosser is also essential for successful flycasting. In many streams, small panfish are hooked so frequently they become a nuisance. This nuisance can be minimized by going to streamers, feathered minnows or grasshoppers tied or moulded on large #2 hooks.

Tips On Bait Fishing

All baits previously recommended for stream bass should be fished alive. This requires that they be transported in efficient containers, then hooked properly and cast gently.

Of all baits recommended, minnows are most difficult to keep alive. If the angler is fishing a stream by boat, he can keep his minnows in good shape by carrying along a large minnow bucket and changing the water frequently. However, it is rarely practical for the angler wading a stream to drag along a large minnow bucket. When wading a stream, it is usually more practical to carry along the hardier live baits. Salamanders, crayfish, frogs and hellgrammites can all be kept alive by transporting them in any small cardboard container filled with damp moss or grass. Such containers fit easily in a small creel. Small holes should be punched in the container to provide plenty of air, and the interior of the container should be kept cool by occasionally dipping the container into the stream.

Recommended baits are best kept alive by hooking them in the following manner: (1) hook minnows through the lips or well above the backbone between midsection and tail; (2) hook salamanders through the roof of the mouth and an eye socket; (3) hook crayfish through the tail near the body; (4) hook hellgrammites under the collar on top of the back near the head. Using small-diameter, light-wire hooks also helps keep all these baits alive. And using hooks of small size (#4's are large enough) also helps keep baits alive and minimizes snagging on the bottom.

All live baits are usually most effective when cast upstream and allowed to drift downstream with the current. When fishing in this manner, a split shot just large enough to provide casting weight should be clamped on the line about a foot above the bait. Of course, repeated upstream casting, even when casts are kept gentle, result in frequent loss of fragile baits; therefore, a large quantity of bait is required for sustained periods of this type fishing.

During most stream conditions, all recommended baits also are effective for stream bass when fished still, and this type of fishing does not require a large supply of baits. This is the one

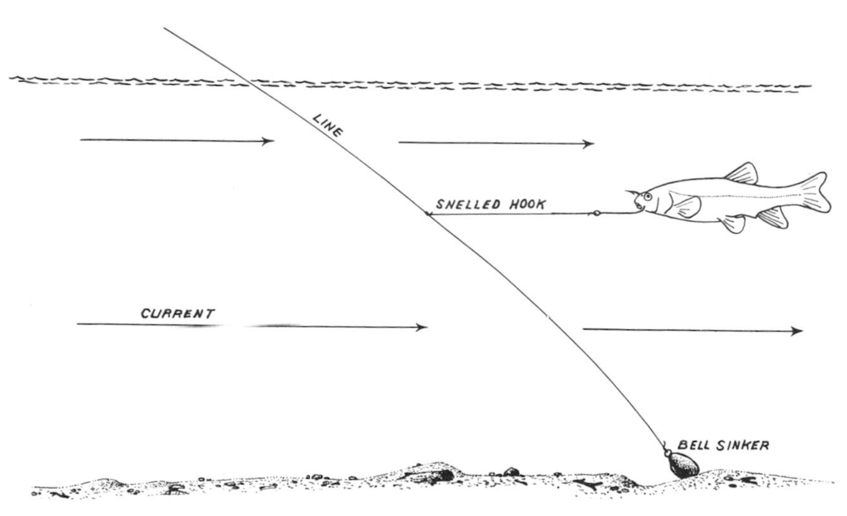

Bottom-fishing bait rig.

type of fishing for stream bass which is effective when conducted downstream. To rig effectively for this type of fishing, the angler should position a weight on the end of his line just heavy enough to hold the bait on the bottom against the current. Then he should attach a snelled hook to his line about eighteen inches above the weight and hook on his bait in the manner just recommended. Casts should be made downstream to those lunker lairs in deep shady water as previously described. The bait should be left on the bottom for long periods; the line should be kept taut and the hook should be set a few seconds after the bass makes a good run.

When fishing in this manner, it is important to keep the boat anchored or tied to a tree limb, or to fish from a position on the bank which is well upstream from the lunker lair being fished for sharp-eyed bass can see a long way upstream!

CHAPTER 3

A Super System for Lunker Bluegills

LUNKER BLUEGILLS can be as temperamental about striking as any bass or trout, and they certainly can be one of the most difficult of all fish to locate. Small bluegills, of course, are a cinch to locate and catch any time, but to take strings of big black oversize bulls with any consistency is a monumental task. A one-two punch with flies and bait, executed skillfully, is most likely to make this feat attainable . . . during the spring or summer months, and whether the old bulls are on or off the beds.

Best Equipment For Big Bulls

The one-two punch against big bluegills is most effective when delivered with cane pole and flyrod, rather than with flyrod alone. Of course, bait as well as flies can be fished with the flyrod, but having the flyrod always rigged with flies and a long and light cane pole always rigged for bait fishing has several distinct advantages.

First, any bait usually will be taken best by big bluegills when it is fished with a cork holding it just off the bottom; and a cork rig is mighty clumsy to use on a flyrod.

Second, live crickets and freshwater shrimp are the number one bluegill baits. These baits are fragile and easily killed or whipped off the hook by casts with the flyrod; but with the old cane pole they can be eased into the water gently at a considerable distance from the boat. Finally, as will be pointed out later, lunker bluegill success usually requires a lot of test fishing with both flies and bait before the big bull's location and preference of the day is determined. Having separate fly and bait outifits always ready at your side makes it easy to switch from one punch to the other, or even to deliver both at the same time.

Any flyrod equipped with any reel will do the job on bluegills, if the line is properly matched to the rod. However, flyrods in the 7 or 8 foot length range are light and less tiring to handle during a long day's fishing. And single-action reels are better than automatics, also because they are lighter and easier on the arm.

Of course, short light rods do not handle heavy popping bugs very well, but who needs wood or even cork-body poppers for bluegills? If the big bulls will take artificials at all, they can be taken in any waters on one of four easy-to-cast flies:

(1) The new life-like plastic or old conventionally-tied willow fly imitations . . . on a # 8 hook.

(2) Green or orange foam-rubber-body crickets with long white rubber legs . . . on a # 8 hook. (These crickets float normally, but can be made into slow-sinkers by squeezing the air out of them below water.)

(3) White or gray slow-sinking rubber-body spiders with long rubber legs . . . on a # 12 short-shank hook.

(4) Life-like plastic red or black fast-sinking ants . . . on a # 10 hook.

A seven-foot level leader of 4 pounds test works fairly well with all the above flies; however, a tapered leader with a 3 or 4 pound test tippet casts all these flies easier and does the job in all but extremely clear water. In air-clear water, it is sometimes necessary to go all the way down to a one-pound-test tippet to take wary bulls. Level fly lines are also adequate. Floating lines work

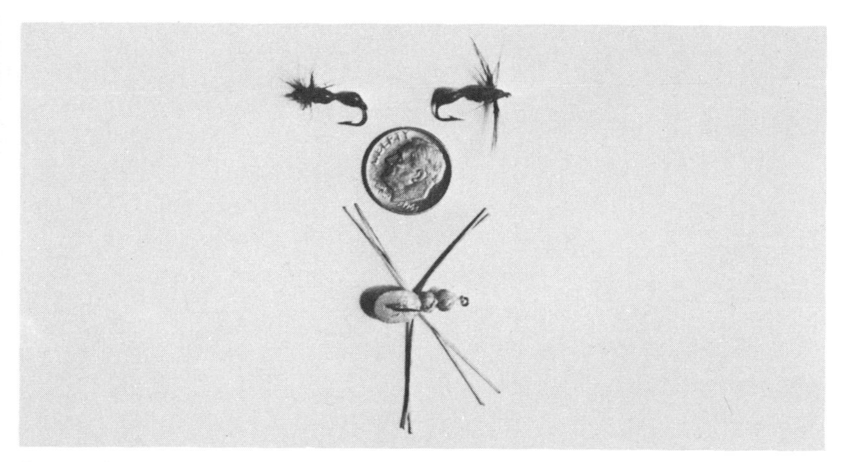

Fast-sinking plastic ants and floating rubber-body crickets are top flyrod offerings for lunker bluegills.

best except when fishing very deep with ants or spiders. Then sinking lines are best. It is best to carry along a reel equipped with each on trips when both shallow and deep fishing may be required.

Cane poles have come a long way in the past few years. Now bamboo poles are widely available in optimum 14 or 15 foot lengths which are so light they feel like good flyrods. These modern poles are highly polished with hard finishes, and last months without cracking. Furthermore, at most good tackle stores, you can pick up one of these super poles with pole-length nylon line, hook, tiny cork, split-shot sinker and # 8 hook, plus a metal and rubber hook-holder on the butt, all at nominal cost.

Finally, a word on baits. If you can get them, live crickets or freshwater shrimp are the best of all big bluegill baits in nine situations out of ten. This is supported by many tests where worms were fished against crickets and shrimp in many sections of the country . . .when thc big bulls were on the beds and off. In every case, crickets or shrimp proved far more deadly on the big bulls.

Modern bait suppliers stock handy throw-away cricket boxes, complete with screen windows and a hole that can be opened by twisting the top to allow only one cricket at a time to come out. Freshwater shrimp are rarely available commercially, but with special equipment, the angler can obtain his own (See chapter 5). If you can't obtain crickets or shrimp, take along a can of live earthworms for your bait punch.

Mobile Fishing For Big Bulls

Being armed with the two-punch bait and flyfishing gear just discussed provides the big bluegill chaser with maximum flexibility in tackle, but mobility is also important. In most waters and during most seasons of the year, moving slowly and quietly along, and steadily test-fishing as you go, is another big key to locating oversize bluegills.

Waders and a floating innertube rig are ideal for small stream and pond bluegill fishing expeditions.

There are two major exceptions to the "keep moving rule." When the location of a bluegill bed is known, it then pays to remain in one place and to fish the bed for long periods. This subject will be discussed in detail in sections which follow. The other exception is when a big willow-fly hatch occurs in the waters you're fishing. Then it pays to anchor the boat within easy fishing distance of an area where the water is being lathered white by feeding fish. While the feeding activity is taking place, either of the willow-fly imitations previously recommended will provoke a charge nearly every time it is cast. Of course, you'll probably take several species of fish in such a situation, but it is likely that a healthy percentage will be big bull bluegills. Then after the surface activity ceases, it pays to stay in the same spot and to go to work with bait.

Now, back to the rule rather than the exceptions. Moving slowly and quietly along, and test-fishing as you go, can be done with a pair of oars or by single-paddle sculling; however, a silent electric motor makes this fishing really mobile and easy. For this kind of fishing, it's hard to beat a boat with a foot-controlled, bow-mounted electric kicker.

Most big bull bluegills which are not spawning or gorging themselves on willow flies are scattered and can only be harvested effectively by fishing as you move along. The pay-off trick in this kind of fishing is to keep moving, and to keep changing flies, and to try bait until you get results. While fishing in this manner, it pays to work the shallows for a period, then water of medium depth, then deep water. Even in the hot months, when some big bulls are bedding in the shallows, others will be scattered about in medium-depth or deep water. Of course, very early in the spring when sun-warmed shallows are the only really warm water in a lake, big bull fishing efforts should be concentrated there.

Rubber crickets or spiders are ideal flyrod offerings for test-fishing the shallows. And no fly will beat a fast-sinking ant for extracting big bulls from medium-depth or deep water.

Bait can be fished effectively in water of any depth. The important point to remember when bait fishing for big 'gills is to keep the cork positioned so that the bait rides just off the bottom. While shoreline test fishing with either flies or bait, it pays to concentrate on areas with shadowy cover, such as grass, trees, lily pads, submerged brush, weeds or rocks.

You can increase your odds for connecting with big bulls by giving them both the fly and bait punch simultaneously; that is, in waters where the use of two fishing sticks is legal. While moving along and shallow-water fishing with artificial crickets or spiders, it pays to "troll" baits in medium-depth or deep water on a cane pole protruding from behind the boat . . . or as the pole is used for shallow-water bait fishing. It pays to troll ants on the flyrod behind the boat.

Persistent mobile fishing with this one-two punch system is almost certain to reward any angler with a big bull bluegill in a reasonable period of time. And when that first old bull is taken, he then knows the lure or bait most likely to produce that day, and he knows the most promising depth at which to concentrate his further angling efforts.

Whenever a big male is taken from the shallows during possible spawning periods, check the fish for a red or orange throat and for sperm. If these signs of spawning activity are present, ascertain whether or not the bull was on a bed. As will be clarified later, if the water is clear you'll be able to see the bed. If it is murky, test-fish the area carefully where you caught the old bull in accordance with the bed fishing procedures to be detailed shortly.

How To Locate Big Bull Beds

If there's an easy time to catch oversize bluegills, it's when they are on their beds. So, for the serious chaser, a detailed knowledge of bluegill bedding habits is all-important. Bluegills may begin bedding as early as April or May in southern climes and as late as June or July in northern states. Each bed will be occupied, then deserted, then occupied again . . . this repeatedly throughout the summer months.

There is no hard evidence to support any predictable timetable of bluegill spawning habits. However, most beds are occupied during the full- or near full-moon periods. And some bluegill experts are certain that beds are occupied during bright moon periods, but only once each three months. However, bluegills have been observed bedding during dark moon periods, and for two or three consecutive months. In other words, it pays to look for beds anytime you're fishing during the spring or summer months.

Scores of big black males, wearing throat patches of red or orange in most waters, congregate in one limited area to bed. These bedding areas are not only comparatively small, but widely separated. This highlights the futility of "blind" fishing in spots chosen at random when bulls are bedding, and the critical importance of carefully marking each bed location, once known, so that it can be found again.

Beds usually look like white spots on the dark bottom. The whiteness is gravel or rock nests fanned clear of silt by the old males. Beds are almost always in water from one to four feet deep. When a female likes a particular nest, she darts in and lays her eggs and departs immediately. The old male remains and guards the eggs until they hatch. He also chases away all smaller fish with ferocious charges. For this reason, when fishing a bluegill bed, the angler will seldom be bothered by smaller fish.

If there's a bluegill lake or stream in your area where you can see the bottom at three or four foot depths, that's the spot to begin your search for big bulls, for a visual search for beds is fastest. And remember, some waters may be murky one day, but clear the next. Cruise that stream or lake near shorelines. Cruise slowly, use polarized sunglasses and watch for those tell-tale white spots on the bottom. Pay particular attention to shallow points jutting out into deep water and to shallow coves near deep water . . . for few beds will be found a great distance from deep water.

Each time you see a white spot in the shallows, shut off your big kicker, then ease back to it with oars or electric motor. Examine the spot closely. If it consists of adjacent oval depressions fanned out on a gravel or rocky bottom, you can be sure it's a bed. If you observe the bed for five or ten minutes and see no big black bulls on it, the bed is deserted. If the bed is occupied, you'll see the old bulls. Each bed, occupied or not, should be carefully marked so that you can find it on return trips to the area. An unoccupied bed may be the place to fish for big bulls on your next trip, or the next year . . . for bluegills tend to bed in the same spots year after year, as well as several times during the summer.

Of course, those mobile test-fishing procedures already discussed usually are necessary to locate beds in murky water. Looking for two subtle bedding signs can help, too. When bluegills are fanning out nests in lily pads, they work the stems of the plants over. This dislodges many small sprouts which float to the surface. And on still days, air bubbles made by males excreting sperm can be seen on the water surface above a bed. A murky water bed located by any of these means also should be carefully marked for future reference.

How To Fish A Bluegill Bed

When an occupied bluegill bed is located, the angler faces only one remaining problem . . . catching the big bulls. But this can be one heck of a job. First of all, the old male's hunger drive is almost nonexistent. They are far more intent on fanning out the nests, guarding them against smaller intruders trying to eat the eggs, and fertilizing each new batch of eggs as females dart in to lay them. Furthermore the crafty old bulls are edgy and easily alarmed by a nearby boat or wade fisherman, by the motion of a pole or rod, or by a line or leader moving around the bed.

Because of these factors, the fisherman must first of all position himself a reasonable distance away from the bed, then fish it quietly and cautiously . . . either by wade fishing or from a boat. This precaution is especially important if the bed is in clear water. As a general rule, you should fish from a point where you can just reach the bed with your cane pole rig, or by a reasonably long cast with your flyrod. To locate such a point with any degree of precision, you must have marked the exact bed location as previously stressed.

The pay-off tactic then is finding out what the critters will take best by slow and deliberate test-fishing . . . then by giving them the preferred morsel in the same fashion. Again, the one-two punch offering of flies, then bait, usually works wonders. Make one or two gentle casts with rubber spiders and rubber crickets. If these are not taken, change to a tiny fast-sinking ant, but

When a big bull is taken, it usually pays to wait at least five minutes before dropping your fly back in the bedding area. This kind of patient fishing will often reward the angler with a stringer full of big bluegills.

remember to go to a one or two pound test leader tippet if the water is clear.

If you take an old bull on any of the fly offerings, ease him in . . .wait at least five minutes and cast again with the same offering. A fly presented in this manner may get you all the bulls you want. On the other hand, flies often will fail, or produce only two or three bulls at the most. In this situation, give the bedding bulls that second punch with bait. As previously stressed, a live cricket or freshwater shrimp is the number one bull bait. But worms will sometimes do the job.

To clean out a bull bed with bait, remember to use a tiny cork and to set it so that the bait rides just off the bottom. Drop the bait in the bedding area with as little water disturbance as possible. Then, hold the pole still and leave the cork in one place for long intervals. You may have to sit in that one spot for several hours to corral a mess of bedding bulls; but if you're willing to pay this price, your rewards are almost certain. As most anglers realize, bluegills are so prolific that the heaviest fishing pressure, even during spawning periods, has no effect on population levels.

Best Times To Fish A Bluegill Bed

The only time to fish a clear-water bluegill bed is during the shadowy hours: early mornings, late afternoons . . . or cloudy, windy or rainy periods. However, big bulls on murky-water beds often will hit during any time of the day and during any kind of weather; that is if they are fished for with patience and with that deadly one-two punch: flies and bait.

CHAPTER 4

Tips for More and Bigger Crappies

CRAPPIES ARE FASCINATING fish. When they first begin to spawn, they are usually two years old and six to eight inches long, but in later years they often attain a length of eighteen inches and a weight of about three pounds in fertile waters. Record fish of four or five pounds have been taken. A seven-inch female crappie will lay about 15,000 eggs, and a high percentage of them hatch! No wonder that biologists have concluded that heavy angling pressure helps rather than hurts most crappie populations.

The main differences in the two species of crappies, the white and the black, are slight variations in coloration, snout length, and dorsal fin arrangement. These differences are of no importance from an angling standpoint. Both species now inhabit the same waters throughout most of the country, and the same angling tactics will take both species. It doesn't take brawn or hard work to catch crappies, but the greatest measure of success will be enjoyed by anglers who stay up-to-date on the most potent angling tactics.

Baitfishing for Crappies

Three basic rules work wonders when baitfishing for crappies: (1) Drift across the deepest holes in the lake with your minnow dragging near bottom until you catch a big crappie; then you'll have a school of respectable fish located; (2) anchor your boat over this hole and fish with a light rod or hand line so you can feel those characteristic light bites of even the big boys; and (3) use the smallest minnows you can get if you want to catch the biggest crappies.

These same tactics will pay off on the big stream as well as on the big lake. When fishing in this manner, a light monofilament line, two # 6 hooks spaced about a foot apart and just enough split shot to hold the minnows down at the desired depth is the rig that pays off.

One important exception: when crappies are spawning in shallow water, different baitfishing tactics are required. Even then, small minnows are still the top natural bait. But to keep from disturbing the wary quarry in the shallows, it is usually best to anchor the boat or wade to a point where the spawning beds can be reached with a long cane pole, a flyrod, or a casting outfit. Than a small cork or bubble, a split shot and a # 6 hook set just deep enough to keep the minnow off the bottom usually adds up to the only tackle combination required to fill the stringer.

When exploring the shallows of a new lake or stream in search of a crappie bed, ease along in either a boat or floating innertube and spot-fish the shallows with small minnows until that first tattle-tale crappie hits. Remember that crappies bed in water that is usually three to twelve feet deep; water that's a bit deeper than that which bluegills and most other panfish bed in. Also concentrate the search for crappies in water filled with logs, stumps, or brush. Test-fishing with these tips in mind usually makes locating that crappie bed easy.

Crappies also can be taken often by bait fishing from the banks of lakes and streams. When the old panfish king is holed up in deep water, the bank fisherman must usually depend upon one of the long-range casting outfits to reach his quarry. In this situation, some lazy-minnow-casting into far-out deep pockets is

When early season crappies are roaming the shallows, wade fishing with jigs, flies or minnows can be highly effective.

a top method for locating the schooling fish. A couple of small minnows on# 6 hooks positioned at foot intervals above a bell sinker, or one of the new floating sinkers, is a good rig to drag those deep bottoms with until you hit that first big crappie. Use a very slow retrieve for this kind of test fishing, and mark well where that first big crappie hits. Then "still fish" that same area with the same rig and you'll often put a big dent in a school of big crappies.

Thus far the small minnow has been recommended as the best all-around bait for crappie fishing, for to do otherwise would be downright dishonest. But, large minnows, worms, and crickets will sometimes take crappies, too, so use these if small minnows are in short supply.

Tossing Hardware for Early Season Crappies

Almost any kind of hardware employed on the end of a spinning, spincasting, or baitcasting outfit will take an occasional crappie, but very small lures are the real super crappie killers. And the best of these are the new "Doodlesockin" jigs. Anglers in Kansas claim to have originated the doodlesockin' technique for catching crappies. The strictest definition of doodlesockin' is "a new technique for extracting crappies from brush-filled waters with new jig-type lures." But in order to doodlesock crappies, they must first be located; therefore, in its broader sense, doodlesockin' also includes new techniques for locating as well as catching crappies.

The New Doodlesockin' Lures

The effectiveness of doodlesockin' is based on one cardinal principle: a very slow-moving, or even still lure will take the most and biggest crappies, provided the lure is sufficiently attractive. As previously indicated, a very slow-moving or still minnow will take finicky crappies the fastest. So will a very slow-moving or still artificial lure if it is appealing enough to the quarry.

Today, there are three new jigs which crappies will literally "eat up," even when the jigs are barely moving. . .and even when they are hanging still in the water. It is these three jigs which make doodlesockin' so effective. These three doodlesockin' jigs will outperform all the older, conventional crappie-jig models. These three top new doodlesockin' jigs are: the Ward Beetle, the Ward Crappie Buster and the Furman Bugg Eye Shiner.

Almost any kind of hardware employed on the end of a spinning, spincasting or baitcastin will take an occasional crappie, but very small lures with rubber body are the real crappie kil

The Beetle, available in weights of 1/64 to 1/4 ounce, is the most revolutionary new crappie jig of the three. This round-head jig has a soft rubber body with a split tail. The body is make of extremely soft rubber; this increases the buoyancy of the jig and it is so appealing in looks and feel to crappies that they often swallow the jig completely. . .even when it's dead still! The Beetle is available in many colors, but tests indicate the white and yellow color patterns are the most consistent crappie producers. The Beetle is available with or without a new plastic weedless device called the "Fiber Guard." The weedless model will rarely hang up in brush, but for tender-mouthed crappies the plain-hook model is better.

The Crappie Buster is a bright-colored, little round-head jig with a chenille body and a maribou tail; it's available in 1/32 to 1/8 ounce sizes. And the Bugg Eye Shiner, available in the same sizes, is a round-head, large-eye jig with a maribou body brightened with strands of silver tinsel which add a deadly shimmering brightness to the lure. The white and yellow models of these two jigs are also the most dependable crappie producers.

Locating Crappies, Test-Casting Techniques

Before actual doodlesockin' can begin, crappies must be located. There are effective new techniques for doing this with the jigs just described. The first is a test-casting technique.

Any search for a crappie school, of course, is much easier if the angler is aware of the kind of water in which the fish are most likely to be found. During the spring and fall months (the winter months in the Deep South), crappie schools most often move to comparatively shallow water, usually water from about three to twelve feet deep. During the rest of the year, crappie schools are usually in deep water, often at depths of thirty feet or more. Whether in deep or shallow water, crappies prefer to school in and around brush, tree stumps or other cover. In shallow water, such cover is usually easily detected because it extends above the water level. But in deep water, such cover is usually submerged, cannot be seen and must be located by test fishing or by use of an electronic fish finder. The best system to test-fish

The best new doodlesockin' jig for crappies is the rubber body Ward Beetle in yellow or white (top). The Crappie Buster (bottom) in bright colors is also good.

all quadrants and water levels around the boat, however, is amazingly fast and effective.

First, it requires the use of a jig, like those just discussed, which is highly attractive to crappies.

Second, it is based on presenting the jig in such a manner that it is always very slow-moving and effective every moment, from the time it hits the water until it is lifted from the water.

To cover all quadrants, two cycles of systematic casts are made to all open water completely around the boat. The first cycle of casts consists of short casts of twenty to thirty feet. The second cycle consists of longer casts of about fifty to sixty feet. On each cast, a tight line is held from the moment the jig hits the water until it reaches bottom. This causes the jig to drop slowly downward and toward the boat. If the rate of this "drop" of the jig is slow enough, the jig is an effective crappie magnet as it drops through all water levels from the surface to the bottom. Then by retrieving the jig very slowly, other water levels arc effectively covered. . .near bottom at the beginning of the retrieve, then medium-depth water, then shallow water as the jig approaches the boat.

The rate of "drop" of the crappie jig is all important when employing the test-casting technique just discussed. This rate of "drop" which must be very slow, is a function of line diameter as well as jig weight. Following are some guidelines which will help in selecting best jig-line combinations to achieve the correct rate of "drop." Lines used in the example are new, small-diameter-for-test lines, such as Bonnyl, Blonde, Stren and 7000 Mono.

Best Jig-Line Combinations For Crappie Fishing

Line Test	Jig Weight
2 lb.	1/64 oz.
4 lb.	1/32 oz.
6 lb.	1/16 oz.
8 lb.	1/8 oz.
10 lb.	1/4 oz.

The ultra-light jig-line combinations are a lot of fun to fish with. However, the crappie fisherman who uses them must expect to spend a lot of time trying, usually without success, to loosen his jig from snags. The heavier jig-line combinations recommended above, at least up to the 8 pound test line and the 1/8 ounce jig, will take crappies fast enough under most situations, and with this combination jig hooks can often be sprung loose from snags. And, for that all-out doodlesockin' in thick brush to be discussed later, the heavier jig-line combinations enable the angler to "well-rope" his fish into the boat before they have a chance to wind the line around snags.

It should also be mentioned that crappies can be caught, although not as fast, with jigs a size larger than those recommended above for the various lines. Going to a jig a size larger than recommended will, of course, increase the rate of "drop" beyond the optimum; however, when test fishing very deep summertime waters, this is sometimes a smart price for the angler to pay to minimize the time he has to wait for the jig to drop down to where the crappies are.

Locating Crappies, The "Poke" Fishing Technique

This crappie-locating technique is a quick and effective method for locating schools of slab-sides when the schools hole up in areas of thick trees and brush. . .as they often do during the spring months, particularly during the spawning periods.

This shallow-water test-fishing technique also requires the use of jigs, like those previously discussed, which are highly attractive to crappies, and an electric trolling motor to propel the boat very slowly through the thick brush and trees. The trick is to poke the rod tip into each brushy area as the boat eases past it and to let the jig slowly down into the brush by releasing line. If a crappie does not gobble down the jig by the time it reaches bottom, then the jig is lifted straight up to avoid snagging, and the next brushy area is "poke" fished in the same manner. When a crappie takes the slow-dropping jig, this usually signals the location of a school and true doodlesockin' can begin.

The True Doodlesockin' Technique

True doodlesockin' is the fastest of all methods, including the use of minnows, for putting crappies in the boat once a school is located! This technique is deadly in brushy, snag-filled water where crappie schools are most often found. It works equally well when fishing deep submerged brush piles during the hot months and when fishing shallow brushy or snag-filled waters in the spring or fall.

The first requirement is to fix the position of the boat directly over that crappie school located by test-fishing procedures just discussed. When possible, each end of the boat should be tied to a tree limb. In deep, treeless water, the boat should be positioned over the school by dropping one anchor on a long rope, well to one side of the school, then easing the boat well to the other side of the school and dropping the other anchor. Then, by taking up the proper amount of slack in the anchor ropes, the boats's position can be fixed directly over the school and the anchors and ropes will not spook the fish or interfere with doodlesockin'.

True doodlesockin' is dropping the jig straight into the brush or snag-filled water where the crappie school is located, manipulating the jig in such a fashion that it catches crappies fast, yet does not snag often. There are several important tricks to executing this technique successfully. First, as already emphasized, to catch crappies fast, the jig must be fished very slowly or still. . .

and only jigs, like those already described, which are highly attractive to crappies, will catch crappies when fished very slowly or still.

Second, to minimize snagging, the jig must be let straight down into the brush, maneuvered only in straight up and down motions, and retrieved straight up to the boat. Any jig drop, jig maneuvering, or jig retrieve which is not straight up or down is likely to result in a snag and a waste of time in attempting to loosen it.

When using highly attractive crappie jigs and effective jig-line combinations like those recommended, and when the angler is over a good crappie school, the jig will probably be inhaled by a crappie the moment it drops to the depth occupied by the school. However, it is well to mark the exact depth at which the first strike occurs, for if the fish do get a little finicky later on, they can often be taken best by simply holding the jig still at that depth, or by giving it an occasional and very slight straight-up jerk.

The exact depth at which the strike occurs is best marked by hand-line fishing. Simply hold on to the line with the thumb and forefinger when the hook is set. . .and use your other fingers on that hand and the other hand to "well rope" the fish in.

As previously indicated, when doodlesockin' in thick brush, many fish are likely to tangle around limbs unless the angler really throws the power to them and really "well ropes" the fish straight up to the boat. This is best accomplished by going to the heavier jig-line combinations previously recommended. When the angler gets directly over a really good crappie school, the larger jigs recommended are usually plenty effective. Of course, because of their comparatively tender mouths, some crappies will tear loose when "well roped;" however, losses are fewer than occur because of fish tangling the line around snags when light lines are used.

Using the true doodlesockin' technique, including the jigs and jig-line combinations just described, the crappie chaser will outfish minnow fisherman in the same boat. This is probably because time isn't wasted reaching for bait and placing it on the hook, and because swimming minnows are bad about snagging hooks in brush.

Modified Doodlesockin' Techniques

The bank fisherman will often be able to locate crappie schools, especially in the spring and fall in most of the country, and during the winter in the Deep South, by employing the same general test-casting techniques explained earlier. Once a school is located and its depth confirmed, a highly effective modification to the true doodlesockin' technique is the use of a bubble or cork above the jig to keep it at the correct depth. If there's a good wind blowing, simply casting to the area occupied by the school and allowing the waves to move the cork and jig will often produce easy and big strings of crappies. When there's no wind, reeling the cork in slowly for a foot or two, then leaving it still for a couple of minutes before reeling again, is also an effective method for nailing crappies, especially big ones.

CHAPTER 5

The Super Bait for Panfish

DOZENS OF KINDS OF freshwater shrimp are found in freshwater lakes and streams from coast to coast. All these shrimp look much like their salt-water cousins, except that they are much smaller. The freshwater shrimp is not much larger than a man's fingernail and not much wider than a pencil lead. They are so tiny that most men have never seen them. . .yet in many waters they constitute the main diet of big bluegills, and they are relished by all panfish as well. Therefore, when fished properly, freshwater shrimp can be one of the most deadly of all panfish baits. They will usually outfish worms, crickets and all other conventional baits.

Equipment for Shrimp Collecting

The freshwater shrimp is so fragile and tiny that a fantastic number of them are required to provide bait for a few hours' fishing. So, the first requirement for successful shrimping for panfish is securing large quantities of bait. Two bait-collecting tools are required for this job.

The basic shrimp-gathering tool is a strong and heavy all-metal net. The hollow steel handle of the net should be six or seven feet long. The strong steel hoop should be about four feet square (2′ by 2′) and should be covered by strong screen-wire mesh. It is best to secure the wire mesh to the hoop with wire so that it is flush with the face of the hoop. The weight of the net makes it easy for the user to slam it through a carpet of thick hyacinths or down into thick grass clumps. The strength of the net keeps the hoop from bending. The flush wire face on the hoop makes most big plant and weed clumps slide off when the net is whipped rapidly through the water, yet it collects the small shrimp.

The second essential shrimp-gathering tool is an effective bait-collector, container and shrimp sorter. This device is a wooden box larger than the net. The sides of the box should be about four inches high. The open top should be covered with heavy gauge screen with 1/4 inch mesh. When the net contents are dropped on the screen, the small shrimp fall into the box, yet most weeds and other debris remain on top of the screen and can be easily brushed away. This assures a quick box of debris-free shrimp. The screen on top of the box should fold back so the shrimp can be easily reached when fishing begins.

Constructing efficient tools, like those just described, is an essential starting point in getting enough freshwater shrimp to fish with; but the shrimp must still be located and the tools used properly.

Where to find Freshwater Shrimp

In areas where floating hyacinths are plentiful, freshwater shrimp usually are plentiful, too. They are most often concentrated in the spongy roots of these plants. Shallow bottoms under water lilies and shallows where weeds or grasses are thick are often shrimp magnets, too. Shrimp tend to congregate in fantastic numbers in small areas. So, the main key to getting adequate numbers of shrimp is to keep moving and netting in the kinds of cover just described until you hit a shrimp concentration. Then you can probably load your bait box in a hurry.

Florida guide baits hook with freshwater shrimp for cane pole fishing for bluegills in thick floating hyacinths. Shrimp box has screen bottom.

In most southern waters, shrimp concentrations can be located any time during the year. In colder waters, shrimp concentrations usually start showing up in the spring and are around throughout most of the summer and fall. And when water conditions are the same, you'll probably find shrimp concentrations in the same place at the same time year after year.

Freshwater shrimp are amazingly fast little critters, so make those swipes with the net fast! If you're netting in floating hyacinths, plunge the net just under the plants and scoop upward as rapidly as possible. Scoop the bottoms under lily pads or in weeds or grasses equally fast.

Often, an area of shrimp concentration discovered while netting bait is also a top fishing area. Since the shrimp are concentrated in the area, fish may also be found close by. Your netting operation also acts as a chumming operation by dislodging and stirring up the shrimp. Fishing areas where shrimp netting pays off can be very productive. . .but shrimp can also be the hottest of all baits when fishing for panfish anywhere.

Fishing Through Hyacinths and Heavy Aquatic Growth

Since fishing under masses of hyacinths or other water plants is not discussed in other chapters, this subject will be briefly treated now.

A specialized tool is essential for fishing through thick, matted hyacinths. This tool is a strong wooden pole about eight feet long. It should have a short metal blade mounted on the end at right angles to the pole. This pole is used to beat holes through the hyacinths to clean an area for fishing. Each hole is beaten with the end of the pole and the metal blade is then used to cut or pull out hyacinths which remain in the hole.

Limber, but strong, cane poles about eight feet long are ideal for fishing through the tiny holes in floating hyacinths, and poles of this length are not in the way when carried in a boat. Strong lines are required to horse big panfish up through the thick plants, but lines of excessive diameter cut down on the frequency of strikes when fishing with the small shrimp. An eight pound test monofilament line is a good compromise. It may sound strange, but it is best to use a large # 4 hook when fishing with the tiny shrimp. When the shrimp is threaded over the hook point and barb, as it should be, the shrimp body also covers most of the hook curve, but all of the shank and some of the curve is left exposed. This exposure of metal does not cut down materially on strike frequency. Even panfish are more easily hooked with this larger-than-usual hook, and a fish rarely swallows this hook, allowing the release of small fish unharmed. When fishing with this cane pole rig, it is best to use a tiny split shot about six inches above the hook. Without this weight it

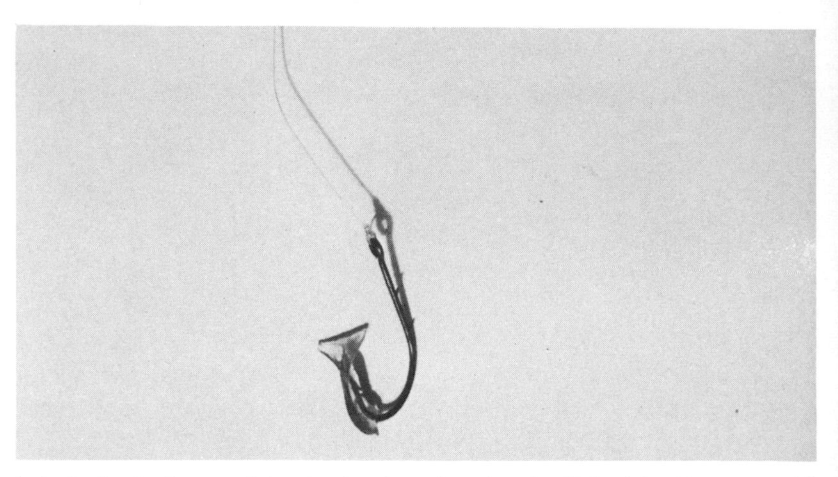

A single tiny freshwater shrimp is placed on the point of a #4 hook in this manner. All panfish will take the shrimp with gusto and without regard to exposed hook shank.

is difficult to sink the bait through the hole in the hyacinths, especially if a wind is blowing.

Most fish under a mass of hyacinths, especially lunker bluegills, feed primarily on shrimp or other aquatic foods which drop downward from the hyacinth roots. Therefore, the best shrimping technique with the cane pole is to let the line down very slowly through the hole, then to keep the bait moving slowly up and down between the base of the floating plants and the bottom.

With that light limber pole, the angler can feel each faint nibble the moment the fish mouths the bait. And when he throws the hook into a big bluegill, shellcracker or crappie, he will really get a workout. Of course, when using a short cane pole the line can't be much longer than the pole and this restricts fishing to a maximum depth of about ten feet. So, when the fish are at deeper levels, a light rod and reel are required when shrimping for panfish. A flyrod or a long light spinning rod with a good reel also makes an ideal shrimping weapon. Lines and leaders should be kept to about eight pounds test and only a very small amount of weight should be used with these rigs, too. The little freshwater shrimp is so fragile that a heavy weight will allow most fish to take the bait off without the angler's feeling a thing.

Hundreds of tiny freshwater shrimp are shown on screen under big shellcracker. These tiny baits can be netted in most waters across the country and are superb baits for all panfish.

Strangely enough, threading the hook with several shrimp will not increase the tempo of strikes. One tiny shrimp on the business end of the hook is just as appetizing, not only to bluegills, but often to crappies and all other panfish as well. Strange, too, is the fact that dead shrimp are just as effective as live shrimp as long as they are kept firm. If the bait box is left out in the sun, the shrimp become mushy, but if the box is kept in the shade, the shrimp will stay firm for several hours, even on a hot day. If frozen while still firm, shrimp can be kept indefinitely and are almost as effective as fresh shrimp when thawed out. Therefore, when the angler finds a good concentration of shrimp, it pays to collect enough to provide bait for several day's fishing.

CHAPTER 6

Walleye and White Bass Super Fishing Systems

THE SHY AND TASTY walleye is a challenging quarry and worthy opponent for any angler. Few fish are as finicky in their feeding habits or as difficult to locate and catch. To score consistently on walleyes, any angler must be a real master in a specialized angling field.

Top Baits And Lures For Walleyes

Although big minnows, big nightcrawlers, big gobs of earthworms and big spoons, spinners, and plugs can be sold to hungry walleyes, they are usually second-rate choices for walleye angling when fishing is tough. Sticking doggedly with large baits and lures probably is the main reason many walleye anglers strike out.

The bait fisherman who wants fast and consistent walleye action should select minnows not exceeding three inches in length, or use just enough worm or nightcrawler to cover a # 6 hook, leaving only about a half-inch of free worm to wiggle beyond the barb.

Small jigs, such as the Doll Fly or Linda Lure, are the best and least used artificial lures for walleyes in most waters. Small spinners, such as the Mepps, and small wobbling plugs, like the Flatfish, run the jigs a close second. 1/4 ounce jigs, in yellow or white, tied with feathers rather than bucktail are usually the hottest walleye producers. 1/6 to 1/4 ounce metal-body spinners, in silver or gold, and one to two inch wobbling plugs in silver, gold, or yellow are the other top lure choices for walleyes. Sure, the use of small baits and lures will result in bothersome strikes from crappies and other panfish, but the angler who sticks with these little "desserts" will clobber the lion's share of big walleyes, too, provided he's fishing in the right water. . .and provided that he's angling correctly.

Where To Fish For Walleyes

The movements of walleyes are controlled primarily by two driving forces: an intense dislike for bright light and a craving for cool, clean water. Of course, the feeding drive is present also, but finicky walleyes usually can find plenty of food within the environments satisfying the two primary forces which control their movements. These factors are the basis for two cardinal rules for determining the best water to fish for walleyes: (1) during the bright, hot hours, the best walleye water usually is deep pockets in lakes or deep holes in rivers; and (2) during the dark, cool hours, shallow shelves or shallow points usually are the top walleye fishing spots.

There is a close relationship between the kinds of water walleyes prefer during the bright hours and during the dark hours. Preferred bottoms usually are clean and sandy both in the deep, bright-hour hangouts, and in the shallow, dark-hour hangouts. Muddy, weedy bottoms should be avoided at all times by the walleye hunter. And the best deep, bright-hour hangouts and the best shallow, dark-hour hangouts are close together, probably because walleyes are both smart and lazy and prefer sections of a lake or stream where they can satisfy all their daily cravings with minimum travel. This fact is an advantage to the angler who appreciates its significance, for once he locates either a bright

-hour or a dark-hour walleye hangout, he knows the other is also nearby.

During walleye spawning time in the spring, rivers and streams entering good walleye lakes are always top spots for lunker walleye action. In lakes without flowing inlet streams, the big spawners frequently are found near the base of rocky dams.

The walleye hunter who heads for the lake or stream with the best baits and lures, and who knows where to look for walleyes, is well on his way to filling his stringer with one of the tastiest fish that swims; however, for high scoring odds, he also must be a student and master of sound walleye angling tactics.

During the spring months, king-size walleyes and white bass are often concentrated along rocky dam faces. Then, small spinners, jigs and plugs are highly effective.

Walleye Trolling Systems

Trolling is a top method for locating schools of elusive walleyes because it enables the angler to cover far more water faster than does any other angling method. And once a walleye school is located, repeated trolling passes through the area often will fill the stringer in a hurry.

Troll slow for walleyes! Whether the walleye angler is trolling deep or shallow, during the bright hours or during the dark hours, the "troll-slow" rule is essential for surest results. Most anglers are inclined to troll far too fast for walleyes, probably because they remember fast action from other fish produced by medium-speed trolling. Walleyes are far lazier than most fish and they will rarely chase a lure moving at medium or fast trolling speeds.

Troll deep during the bright hours and shallow during the dark hours. This is the second tactic for clobbering walleyes. As already emphasized, it's in deep holes and pockets where the big schools of walleyes usually hang out during the bright, sunshiny hours; so then, it's way down deep where the lure should be trolled. And it's on those shallow shelves and points where walleyes are most often found during the dark hours; so, when trolling early in the morning, late in the afternoon, and on dark, cloudy days, a shallow-riding lure most often pays off.

There are several tricks for proper trolling with those top walleye lures already discussed. To make the deadly little jig or spinner ride shallow while trolling, only a single lure should be trolled on the line, no additional weight should be used, and the trolling line should be kept short. Both jigs and spinners can be made to ride deep by trolling with a long line and by adding weight a few feet ahead of the lure. Jigs are often most effective for deep trolling when jigs spaced a couple of feet apart are used in lieu of the added weight.

Walleyes usually cruise near the bottom both when they are in their shallow, dark-hour hangouts and when they are in their deep, bright-hour hangouts; so, as a rule, the jig or spinner is being trolled slow and deep enough only when it occasionally touches bottom. But no lure is effective when dragging moss or weeds. Therefore, lures should be checked frequently to make certain they are clean. Since frequent snagging must be expected when trolling properly for walleyes, jigs and spinners with light wire hooks and lines strong enough to straighten out those hooks are highly desirable.

To be effective against walleyes, spinners may be trolled at an even speed, but jigs must be trolled with a series of slow jerks. Few summer walleyes will be taken on any jig trolled at an even speed.

Floating models of the small wobbling plugs recommended earlier are highly versatile walleye trolling lures. When no weight is used, these little plugs are excellent for shallow trolling. And when properly weighted, they may be trolled at a constant level just above deep bottoms. For constant-level, deep-water trolling, a two or three ounce bell sinker should be tied on the end of the trolling line; the little plug should be fastened to one end of a three-foot leader, and the other end of the leader should be tied to the line about four feet above the sinker. When trolling slow with this rig, the sinker will bounce along the bottom and the lure will ride just above the bottom. In most walleye lakes, there is no better bottom trolling rig, especially if the angler is trolling across those clean sandy bottoms where most walleyes hang out.

Best Walleye Casting Systems

Once a school of walleyes is located, concentrated casting in that area from bank or boat will often produce a limit of fish. As already indicated, trolling likely walleye water usually is the fastest method for locating a walleye school. But the angler without a boat must locate his walleye school by test-casting from the bank. This test-casting should be carefully restricted to those most likely walleye waters described earlier.

Retrieve the lure slow and near the bottom. This is a cardinal rule for successful walleye casting from bank or boat, and it applies regardless of the type of lure being used and when fishing either shallow or deep water. If the caster will stick to a six or eight pound test line, he can cast 1/4 ounce jigs or spinners with any good spinning or baitcasting outfit far enough to catch fish. When casting these lures to either shallow or deep water walleye hangouts, the lure should be allowed to sink to the bottom before

Once a school of walleyes is located, concentrated casting to that area with slow-moving jigs will often guarantee a quick limit of fish.

the retrieve is started. Spinners should be retrieved just fast enough to feel the blade turning. Jigs should be bounced slowly along the bottom by a series of sharp, widely-spaced jerks. When using one of the small wobbling plugs, it will be necessary to add about 1/4 ounce weight, preferably a clamp-type sinker, to the line about two feet above the plug. This type plug should be retrieved just fast enough to keep it off the bottom. The slow retrieve should be continued even as the lure approaches the bank or boat, for walleyes will often follow the plug and strike it at their last opportunity.

Keep changing lures. Any one of the super walleye lures already recommended may be the best walleye producer on any given day. Therefore, the caster should keep changing lures until he establishes which one generates the most action. Also, when a walleye school is located, the fish often will cease striking a single lure after it takes a few fish, and a new lure may take more fish from the school.

When the action's slow, sweeten the lure. A small minnow or piece of worm or night crawler on the hook behind a jig or on the treble hook of a spinner is a deadly tactic for taking walleyes when fishing's tough. And a small piece of worm on the treble hook of a little wobbling plug often will take walleyes when nothing else will.

Best Walleye Baitfishing Systems

Small baits fished in the right water at the right times, as already defined, are always super walleye producers. Small baits should be fished on small hooks. Long-shank #6 hooks are large enough for walleyes. An inch-and-a-half minnow hooked through the lips on a # 6 hook will make the desired lively presentation which interests finicky walleyes. And a piece of worm or nightcrawler just large enough to cover a long-shank # 6 hook with a half-inch of free worm to spare is just the right size for walleyes.

Fish minnows and worms in combinations. No angler can predict whether walleyes will prefer a minnow or a worm on any given day; therefore, on each line two hooks should be used, one baited with a minnow and the other with a worm. After the bait preference is determined, then that bait should be used on both hooks.

Use a float when fishing the dark-hour shallow water hangouts. Baits riding just above the bottom produce the fastest walleye action. When fishing shallow water, the use of a cork or bubble is the best way to achieve this bait depth. The cork or bubble should be heavy enough to provide the weight required for casting, and only a tiny split shot should be used to keep the minnows or worms down. The cork should be set so the bottom hook rides just above the bottom. The split shot should be clamped on the line above the bottom hook. The upper hook, on a six-inch snell, should be fastened to the line about 18 inches above the bottom hook.

Use a bottom-fishing rig when fishing the bright-hour, deep-water hangouts. When fishing deep water, the use of a float is not practical and a bottom-fishing rig is required. The objective of the bottom-fishing rig for walleyes should also be to keep the baits off the bottom. This can be accomplished by using about an ounce of weight against which a taut line may be maintained. The first hook, on a six-inch snell, should be fastened to the line about 18 inches above the sinker, and the second hook, also on a six-inch snell, should be fastened to the line about a foot above the first hook. By maintaining a taut line from bank or boat, hooks rigged in this manner will usually ride just above the bottom.

Keep the bait moving. A moving bait will produce the most walleye strikes. When using a cork, the bait should be reeled in slowly for a few feet every few minutes. When bottom fishing from the bank, the same procedure should be used. When bottom fishing from a boat, letting the boat drift slowly along with the sinker dragging the bottom is a top method for locating a walleye school. Once the school is located, the boat should be anchored and repeated casts and slow retrieves across the bottom will stir up the fastest walleye action.

The Combo Rig—New White Bass Slayer

Small spoons, spinners or jigs will take an occasional white bass when they are striking well, but a hot new rig will usually take them faster than any conventional offering. This deadly new white bass slayer is called the Combo Rig. It works wonders on bull whites in deep and shallow water, in spring, summer or fall.

The shallow water Combo Rig is a tiny jig trailing 18 inches behind a noisy topwater plug. Using this rig is like using dynamite whenever whites are feeding just below the surface. And it is quick magic for ending those frustrating periods of fruitless casting to whites which are lathering the surface after bait fish, but which won't hit a conventional lure.

For best results, it is essential that the trailing jigs of the Combo Rig be the same size as the minnows the whites are feeding on. Very tiny 1/64th or 1/32nd ounce jigs, such as the Ward Crappie Buster, are best when fish are charging newly-hatched schools of very tiny minnows, such as spring or early summer shad. Later in the season as the minnows grow larger, 1/16th or 1/8th ounce jigs, such as the Crappie Buster or Doll Fly, usually are best. Watch those minnows jumping ahead of your quarry, or examine those in the stomach of the kind of fish you're after, then match the size of those minnows with your trailing jig.

Big, noisy surface plugs, such as the Lucky 13, used ahead of the jig, helps generate the fastest Combo Rig strikes, probably because the noise such plugs make attracts white bass feeding on or near the surface. Spinner-type topwater plugs are a nuisance to use as the spinners cause bothersome tangles of the trailing leader. Even less tangles occur when the hooks are removed from the lead plug and when the leader holding the jig is attached to the rear screw eye; however, when the angler removes the plug hooks he forfeits his chance to take an occasional lunker bass on the plug itself. . .and the lunker whites do hit the plug once in a while.

The Combo Rig is also effective when two small jigs are used, one trailing the plug by about a foot and the other by about two feet. No swivels are required with this rig. Light colored jigs, especially whites and yellows, usually work better than dark jigs.

When possible, casts with the surface Combo Rig should be made to the immediate area where schools of white bass are observed surface feeding, and the rig should be retrieved with a series of frequent and sharp jerks. Even when fish are not observed surface feeding, casting shorelines with the Combo Rig often pays off during the early morning and late afternoon hours, not only in white bass, but often in good strings of bluegills and crappies as well.

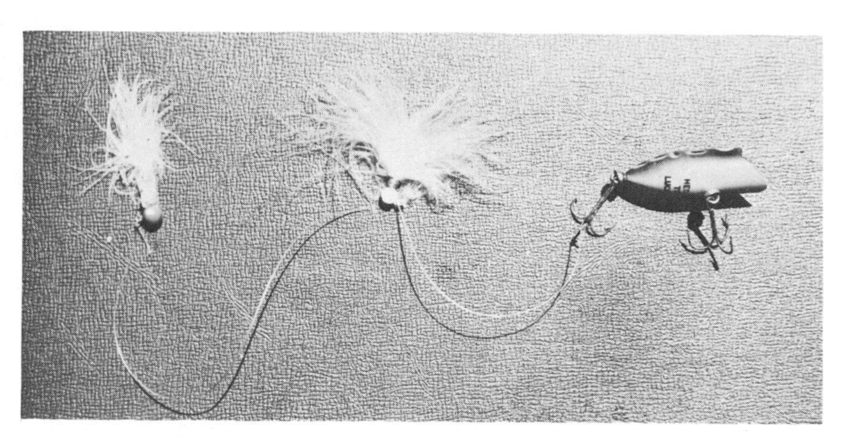

The unusual shallow water combo rig is highly effective when white bass are "on the jump." The Lucky 13-type plug is followed by either one or two small jigs. The deep water combo rig consists of a deep running plug followed by one jig.

When white bass are hugging the deep bottoms, trolling a single jig trailing behind a deep running plug is a highly lethal tactic. This unusual angling method will often produce phenomenal catches of lunker whites.

Big, very deep-running, backward-moving plugs, such as the largest size Bomber, are the best lead lures to use for deep-water fishing with the Combo Rig. White or other light colored Bombers usually produce the best, and take an occasional good fish on their own. Such lures wobble along the bottom and "walk" easily over most rocks and snags.

As in shallow-water Combo Rig fishing, best jigs to use are those matching the size of the minnows the fish are feeding on. And best jig colors for deep fishing with the Combo Rig also are whites and yellows.

While deep fishing with the Combo Rig, it is impossible to keep from snagging the trailing jig on the bottom occasionally. To save the expensive lead plug, the main trolling line should be strong (about fifteen-pound test) and the jig leader should be light (8 or 10-pound test). Good jigs, which ride with hooks up when trolled, such as the Crappie Buster, Doll Fly or Linda Lure, will snag far less frequently than will most cheap jigs.

To save line twists and tangles while fishing the deep Combo Rig, good snap swivels should be used ahead of the lead plug and at the plug end of the trailing jig leader. However, a swivel immediately ahead of the jig reduces the frequency of strikes and is not necessary. Also to save leader tangles, the lower treble hooks of the Bomber-type plug (those nearest the tail) should be removed. The snap-swivel, with leader and jig attached, should then be snapped into the rear screw eye of the plug. That remaining forward treble on the Bomber will still take those occasional fish which strike the plug. The single jig should trail the plug by about three feet.

Solving White Bass Location Problems

Of course, even the hot new Combo Rig will not pay off unless it is fished where the white bass are, and in water where they are hitting best. White bass are spring spawners, so the hottest spots for early season fishing are those moving streams which enter good white bass lakes. Both spring and fall fishing for whites also can be good in the lakes themselves, especially along the steep rocky faces of dams, and over shallow points and in shallow coves with good cover. Spring and fall is white bass "jump time" in lakes everywhere, and the easiest way to locate whites is to watch for areas where they are lathering the water white in pursuit of bait fish.

In very deep impoundments throughout the country, white bass usually go to deep water in the hot summer months. Then white bass fishing is toughest, especially for those who haven't discovered the deep-water Combo Rig. There are lakes throughout the country, however, especially in the South and East, where white bass surface action stays good throughout the summer. These are comparatively shallow lakes with gushing inlet streams, like TVA's Watts Bar. Here, mid-summer waters stay cool and the fish continue feeding on or near the surface, even in the hottest months. Sharp anglers after fast mid-summer white bass action will look precisely for such fishing holes, and they'll remember that the best times to fish such lakes are right after periods of heavy surface-cooling rains.

In comparatively shallow lakes, like TVA's Watts Bar, midsummer waters stay and white bass gorge in the shallows and on the surface much of the year.

CHAPTER 7

Magic for Muskellunge and Northern Pike

THE MIGHTY MUSkellunge has probably broken more lines and more hearts per strike than any other freshwater fish. But no other fish is like a musky. Old "Long Face," as the Indians called him, is a cunning and temperamental lone wolf, relatively scarce and difficult to locate in the best waters. Even the expert musky fisherman usually expects to devote many days of relentless fishing to hook a single musky . . . and he's glad to do it. For once hooked, the musky is a challenging adversary. In brute power and size, he is matched by few game fish. His tricks for extracting hooks and for stealing lures are highly effective and completely unpredictable. And you can be sure he will have plenty of these sneaky tricks up his sleeve. By the time you bring him to gaff, (and you'll need a gaff to handle a big musky), you'll know you've earned your trophy.

Yes, hanging a trophy musky on the wall is no small task. It requires hard and persistent fishing in promising waters, the use of specialized tackle, and the employment of super fishing tactics.

Where To Fish For Muskies

Muskies can now be taken from the Carolinas and Tennessee northward to Canada, and from Minnesota eastward to Maine and New York. They are found in the Ohio and Mississippi River watersheds. But the man who really wants a trophy musky should concentrate his angling efforts in the St. Lawrence River, or in Wisconsin's Hayward area, Lac du Flambeau Indian Reservation, or Chippewa Flowage. Top runner-up bets for giant fish include Minnesota's Lake of the Woods, Michigan's St. Clair River, West Virginia's Elk River and New York's Lake Chautauqua.

In deep weedless lakes, such as Chautauqua, giant muskies usually lurk along gravel or rock bottoms thirty to fifty feet deep, especially in the summer months. In flowing rivers and more shallow, weedy lakes, muskies often prefer water about fifteen feet deep. Typical big musky hotspots in these waters are sandbars and weedbeds near shore, but even better are those well out in lakes. Dropoffs and channels between lakes are great, too. If you have an electronic fish locator, it is a simple matter to find these musky hotspots, even when they are far from shore. This does not mean that big muskies cannot be taken from shallow water. Occasionally they are, especially in the fall months. But deeper waters most often produce the biggest fish. Remember also that big lakes usually are the most promising lairs of big fish.

Best Musky Tackle

When going after a special fish you need special equipment, and musky fishing is no exception. If you are really serious about catching big muskies, you should have a rod capable of fishing for, hooking and fighting a big fish.

The best musky rod is one with a long handle, preferably twenty inches. You'll need this long handle so that you can use two hands for casting the large baits that catch big muskies, to provide the leverage to set the hooks in that massive jaw, and to give the support required to give you a chance in the battle with the giant. A rubber butt on the handle will make two-handed casting easier and cushion your stomach while you are fighting a monster. Several manufacturers make rods with long handles called "musky specials" at slight extra cost. Find a handle that is comfortable for you. Many fishermen use regular saltwater surfcasting rods. These are fine for fighting the fish, but the offset handle of a conventional rod made for freshwater fishing makes casting easier.

The rod should be a stiff, heavy-action model, six to eight feet long, including handle. This type rod provides the leverage required to cast heavy baits long distances and to combat the brute strength of a big musky. Many musky experts use bass-size baitcasting reels, such as the Pflueger Supreme or the Ambassadeur 5000. Even better are baitcasting reels of larger line capacity and strength, such as the Ambassadeur 6000 or Pflueger Rocket.

Twenty-five to thirty pound test lines are optimum for most musky fishing. Either braided nylon or monofilament types will do. Regardless of the type of line you select, a wire leader is a necessity. Without it, even the strongest of lines may be shredded by the musky's super sharp teeth. A 24 inch leader will do for artificial baits, but for live baits, three feet of wire should be used. Lead-core lines are needed when trolling deep for muskies. This subject will be discussed later.

A good musky outfit: A stiff long-handle rod, a high line capacity reel with Star drag and a 27 pound test line, a 24-inch wire leader and a Creek Chub Pikie Minnow plug.

Baitfishing Musky Magic

"The bigger the bait, the bigger the fish." This statement certainly applies to musky fishing. If you want big muskies, use big baits. Muskies have been caught by walleye fishermen who, while fighting a walleye, had a musky strike the hooked walleye. Many crappie fishermen have had a similar experience. This demonstrates the almost unbelievable viciousness and boldness of the great muskellunge.

While it is illegal to use game fish for bait, in most waters suckers are legal and are one of the most effective musky baits. For big muskies, use a twelve to fifteen inch sucker. These are available in most live bait shops in musky areas, or they can be caught on worms in most streams. These baits can be used in one of two ways: rigged for still-fishing or for casting and retrieving like an artificial lure.

Most tackle shops in musky areas have musky hooks that come with a 30 to 36 inch wire leader ready for use with a sucker, or you can make your own rig with a size 6/0 hook and a strong wire leader. To allow the sucker to swim freely while still-fishing, don't just hook it through the head or the back like a minnow. Instead, tie it with fishing line threaded through its back in front of the dorsal fin. Tie the hook securely to the sucker, but not

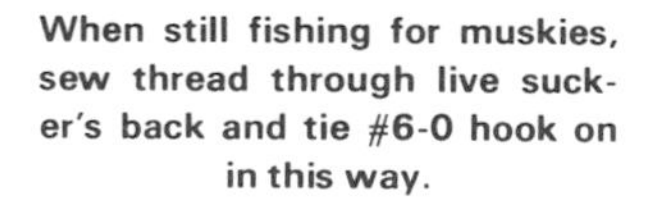

When still fishing for muskies, sew thread through live sucker's back and tie #6-0 hook on in this way.

through it. You'll need a large bobber, the biggest you can get. Don't put a sinker on the sucker. Let it swim freely and seek its own cover.

Still-fishing suckers is an easy way to fish. Just let out about thirty yards of line behind the boat and watch your float. When the musky takes it, just row along following the float. Allow time for the musky to take the sucker in, and to turn it around in its mouth. Sometimes a musky will hold the bait for ten minutes before trying to swallow it. Let the line play out and stop. When it starts to move again, set the hook hard. Many big muskies are lost because the hook is not properly set. That heavy-action rod with the long handle previously recommended is necessary for this job.

Casting suckers in the same manner as artificial lures sometimes pays off when still-fishing fails. For this type fishing, place the hook through the sucker's head. Make sure you've got a secure rig. You'll need both hands to cast the heavy bait. You'll be surprised at the splash the big sucker and cork will create, but that's what often attracts the real granddaddy muskies. The sucker will die after a few casts, but that makes no difference, as you provide all the bait action needed during the retrieve. Cast out with both hands. Now, heave the bait in, allowing your rod tip to go slightly behind you. Then, as you recoil forward toward the bait, reel in. Do this as fast as you can. A musky may take the sucker any time from the moment it hits the water until you are pulling it out of the water for another cast.

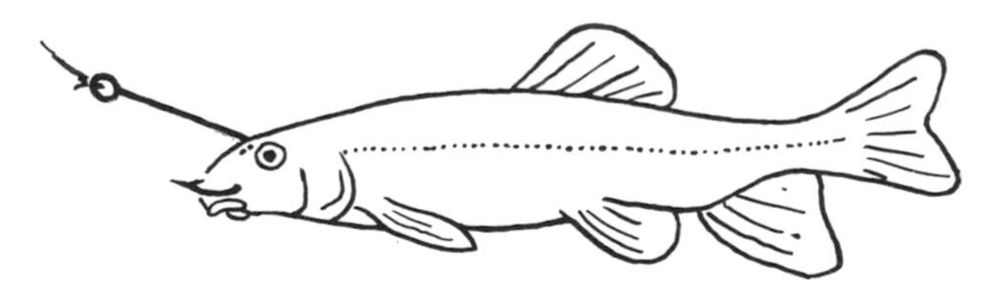

When casting suckers and retrieving them like a plug, hook sucker firmly through head.

When a musky strikes, be careful. Don't set the hook as you would with a plug. Immediately play out slack line and give the musky time to take the sucker, turn it around in its mouth and swallow it. Prior to a strike, you may see a "V" in the water as a musky approaches your bait. If so, don't stop reeling. If anything, speed up your retrieve. This is more likely to make him strike. Once he takes the sucker, sit back; try to think of that bare spot on your den wall, wait until he swallows the bait. Then set the hook with all the might you can muster.

You'll find this type of fishing extremely tiring. It's good practice to condition your arms and back by doing push-ups and pull-ups before attempting a week of hard musky fishing in this manner.

The baitfishing methods just discussed can pay off any time of the year, but they are most effective in the fall months.

Musky Casting Tricks

Casting with artificials is also a top tactic for taking king-size muskies. Casting can pay big dividends in all musky waters, but it is especially effective in the spring and fall in the more shallow and weedy lakes and streams.

The big artificials are also best for big muskies. Big Creek Chub Pikie Minnows in pike-scale finish, and the largest Rapalas and Rebels in silver with dark back probably take more big muskies than all other plugs combined. The old Suick plug, basically a stick with hooks that resembles the sucker with its gray color, is also an effective musky plug. Big spinner and bucktails run the plugs a close second in musky-taking honors. Big silver spinners, such as the Mepps Musky Killer, with black bucktail and red feather, or with an all-red bucktail, will sometimes tease the old tigers into striking when nothing else will.

That same fast heaving retrieve previously recommended for casting suckers is usually the best when casting artificials too. When a musky takes an artificial, he may never surface. He may go straight down. Or, he may dance in a silvery spray like a tarpon, but not as often. He'll try every trick in the book, and then some. He may head for the boat, or from it. He'll probably try to spit the lure in your face. To combat this, you must set the hooks instantly and with great force when he strikes, and keep the hooks set solidly throughout the battle.

Muskies are great followers. They may swim just behind the lure to the boat, and even bump against the boat. When this happens, the trick is to remain calm and to slowly make a figure eight with the lure in the water at the edge of the boat. This may generate a wall of water which drenches you, and a battle which you'll never forget.

Trolling For Muskies

Very slow trolling with head-hooked suckers or with any of the lures just described will take muskies, especially in the spring and fall months. However, in deep musky lakes in mid-summer, deep trolling with lead is often the only way to stir up musky action.

There are two ways to troll with lead. One is to use heavy lead sinkers. This is an inferior way to troll deep because it does not permit the angler to feel the action of his lure or to judge whether or not it is fouled. Using a lead-core line is the best way to troll deep for muskies. This method permits the angler to troll at great depths, to feel the action of his lure and to determine whether or not the lure is fouled. It also permits the hooked fish to fight with far more freedom.

All deep-running lures of the types recommended for casting also are good lures for deep trolling. But Horace McIntyre's "Lake Chautauqua Special" rig is probably one of the hottest of all deep-trolling musky killers. This rig consists of a June Bug Spinner followed by a big Creek Chub Pikie. . .a dark colored Pikie on dark days and a light colored Pikie on bright days. Horace, who has taken more than a hundred legal muskies a year from New York's Lake Chautauqua, confines his summer trolling to depths of 30 to 50 feet. And if he really wants action, he trolls only when the water is choppy.

The Musky Guide

Finally, a word on musky guides. Musky fishing is like big game hunting. If you don't know the water, it may take you a week to locate a fish without help. For this reason, it makes sense to hire a guide when fishing new musky water for the first time. However, don't hire any guide. Make sure to hire a musky guide. Some guides fish for all kinds of fish. There are some, however, who are exclusively musky experts. If you want a better chance of filling that bare spot on the wall in your den, get an all-out musky man. Ask around the bait shops and restaurants. Find out who has the best reputation for getting big fish. Then hire him.

Fish several days with the guide and learn his techniques and the kind of water he fishes. But remember that it's a matter of honor not to return and fish a guide's specific fishing holes without his permission.

Tackle For Northern Pike

The northern pike is one of the most cooperative of all game fish. . .and one of the most abundant. He strikes streamers, lures or baits readily. He thrives in fantastic numbers in most Canadian lakes and in many in Alaska. Most of our northern states offer good pike fishing. And the pike has been successfully introduced in large impoundments in many other sections of the country, especially in the West. Although the pike is not noted for fighting ability or table qualities, some king-size pike will rival the battle put up by a big musky, and pike fillets, although bony, are tasty enough, especially on the stream or lake bank.

Some anglers who gun specifically for monster pike use the same rods, reels, lines, lures, and baits recommended for musky fishing. However, a twelve or fifteen pound test line on a conventional bass reel, such as the Ambassadeur 5000, Zebco's Cardinal 4, the Pflueger Supreme, or the Garcia-Mitchell 510, plus a conventional bass action rod, will do an adequate job on most big pike and are far more fun to use than heavier tackle.

Big wobbling spoons, such as the red and white, silver or gold Dardevle, have probably taken more northerns than all other lures combined. And these streamlined spoons are among the easiest of all lures to cast. Big Mepps spinners and Rebel and Rapala plugs, also in silver or gold, will slay northerns, too. The best flies for northerns are big four to six inch streamers, the brighter and gaudier the better, tied on 2-0 or 3-0 hooks. Of course, casting flies in this size and weight range is tiring, and requires a heavy-action flyrod and a heavy line.

Suckers or any other large minnow will take northerns. Pike are exceptionally cannibalistic. There are lakes in Alaska which have only pike in them. In these lakes, it is not uncommon to dress a big northern and to find smaller pike in its belly.

An eighteen inch light wirc leader ahead of lures and baits is ample when fishing for northerns. Many anglers consider the same length leader in thirty pound monofilament even better.

Tactics For Northerns

The most important key to successful pike angling is knowing the kinds of water to fish during the various seasons of the year. The hottest time to fish for northerns is in the cool spring and fall months. Then most fish are in shallow water 24 hours a day and are easy to locate by simply casting shorelines. Most likely spots are weed beds, rocky areas, and coves with stumps or fallen timber. Shallows between large lakes are exceptionally promising spring and fall fishing bets. In the spring, spawning pike also congregate in feeder streams entering lakes. There is no surer or faster way to take slab-sided northerns than to fish such streams during the early season weeks. Trolling the shallow shorelines with those big gaudy streamers or lures just discussed also is a top northern tactic during the cool months.

When the water heats up in mid-summer, pike become more difficult to locate. Although smaller pike tend to remain in shallow water even then, the real monsters spend much of each hot summer day holed up in deep water. There are several sharp

South Dakota's Oahe Reservoir produced this 22 pound northern. Many western impoundments are now trophy pike producers.

These early season northerns and white bass gobbled up spoons trolled in the shallows of Colorado's Bonny Reservoir.

tricks for digging the old lunkers out. First, remember that big northerns are lazy in the summer. They prefer to hole up in deep, cool and shady water which is adjacent or very near to shallow feeding areas, such as weed beds or rocky coves or dam faces. With a good fish locator, these lunker lairs can be easily spotted. And when the water is clear they often can be spotted visually.

A top tactic is to anchor the boat so that casts can be made to both the deep water and to the nearby shallows. To probe the depths, use a fast sinking spoon or spinner and let it hit bottom before beginning the retrieve. And occasionally move one of these lures, or a plug or streamer, across the adjacent shallows. During this operation, the deep water is most likely to produce. However, a shallow-water cast can pay off, too, for even in the hottest weather northerns will occasionally leave their deep lairs to probe for food in the nearby shallows. In the West, the faces of rocky dams are real hotspots for hot-weather northerns, and this kind of water can be worked effective by bank fishing. The best tactic is to move slowly down the bank working both the shallows against the dam and the straight-out deep water.

A slow retrieve usually pays off when gunning for trophy northerns any time of the year. In the hot months, a slow retrieve is mandatory for success in most waters.

CHAPTER 8

Super Lake-Fishing Systems for Summer Trout

TROUT IN ANY LAKE can be exceedingly difficult to catch in the hot summer months. When lake temperatures rise, trout often won't, and it becomes necessary to locate and dig them out of the bowels of deep lakes or out of mossy caves in shallow lakes. During the hot months, trout in lakes often become finicky feeders. They tend to spurn flies, lures and baits which they strike with gusto during the cooler months. Their urge to feed is then influenced by water, weather and light conditions more than at any other time of the year. For all these reasons, conventional angling tactics are often worthless on the hot-weather trout lake—and super tactics must be employed to trigger trout action. The purpose of this chapter is to summarize those tactics which will work during the tough hot months: tactics which have been proof-tested in both deep and shallow lakes from coast to coast.

Best Times To Fish A Summer Lake

It is possible to extract trout from summer lakes any time; so the best hours to fish are all that you can. However, during certain limited and predictable periods trout in any summer lake are much easier to catch than during other hours, and the angler who is able to concentrate his time and energies on fishing during these "hottest" periods is the one most likely to take big strings of trout.

On summer lakes trout fishing periods which are most likely to be "hot" during daylight hours are: (1) the early morning and late afternoon hours, (2) periods immediately following rain showers, (3) windy periods when the lake surface is rough, and (4) periods when trout are rising to a modest insect hatch. Fishing under lantern light at night also can be highly effective on the summer lake.

On summer lakes, early morning and late afternoon hours, and periods following rain showers are usually the "hottest" trout fishing periods.

(U.S. Bureau of Reclamation Photo.)

Of course, there is no way of proving why trout strike best during these periods. Perhaps it is the subdued light of early mornings, late afternoons, windy periods, and of a lantern at night which stimulate trout to feed, or perhaps the subdued light stimulates more strikes because it makes lines and leaders less visible. Perhaps windy and rainy periods are hot because they tend to cool the lake surface or because they tend to sink floating and flying insects into the water. And it's not difficult to make reasonable guesses as to why trout usually are taken easily when modest insect hatches occur, but not when insect hatches are heavy. Insect hatches stimulate trout to feed, but if the hatch is very heavy and insects dot the water, a fly simply faces too much competition to be taken readily.

The reasons why summer trout strike best during the periods just described are not important, but the fact that they do is. It will pay any angler to keep this fact in mind and attempt to time his assaults on summer lakes accordingly.

Best Lake Areas And Depths To Fish

It is, of course, necessary to determine the location of trout concentrations in order to catch fish. In the large summer lake this usually is a complex problem, except during those infrequent periods when trout are surface-feeding. In the final analysis, lake areas with trout concentrations, and the depths of those concentrations must be determined by effective search and test-fishing techniques. These modern techniques will be discussed in detail later. However, any search for trout in a large lake can be shortened if it is conducted in accordance with these key guidelines:

(1) Lake areas along downwind shorelines are most likely to contain concentrations of summer trout. Much scientific data is now available to support the fact that plankton, the food of most small bait fish, is concentrated in water near the lake surface; that summer winds tend to pile up or concentrate plankton near downwind shores; that schools of bait fish follow the plankton; and that trout concentrations follow the bait fish.

(2) Sections of a lake where current is present, such as areas near stream inlets or outlets, very often hold excellent trout concentrations.

Lake areas along downwind shorelines are most likely to contain concentrations of summer trout.

(3) In shallow lakes, deep pockets in moss and the shady sides of moss or weed banks are usually preferred by summer trout.

(4) Concentrations of lake trout usually are found at depths where the water temperature is between 45 degrees and 55 degrees. Concentrations of rainbows and browns usually will be found at depths where the water temperature is between 60 degrees and 70 degrees.

Best Deep Lake Trolling Systems

In the hot months, sharp trolling is usually the fastest and most effective tactic for locating trout in big deep lakes. The first key trolling trick is to concentrate trolling time in those most promising areas just described.

The second trick is to keep the lure running at those depths where the water temperature is suitable for the kind of trout you're after. A thermometer capable of reading underwater temperatures can be used to quickly determine these most promising trolling depths. The actual depths of trout concentrations, as well as their locations also can be ascertained by scanning as you troll with a good electronic fish-finder. If you are not equipped with either of these modern angling aids, your only recourse is to vary trolling depths until you take a fish, then to continue trolling at that depth.

Three general guidelines can help if you are trolling blind: (1) In most summer trout lakes, except southern impoundments, temperatures preferred by rainbows and browns will usually be found at depths of between five and fifteen feet below the lake surface. (2) In southern impoundments, these preferred temperatures are usually at deeper levels. (3) Temperatures preferred by summer lake trout usually are at depths in excess of twenty feet.

When using a fish locator as an aid while trolling, pay particular attention to indications of bait fish schools near the surface. Any lake area saturated with bait fish should be thoroughly trolled and searched . . . for it is highly probable that a big concentration of rainbows or browns is cruising somewhere just below the bait fish in that area. And, if the lake contains lakers at all, a school of them may well be cruising below the rainbows. I have observed this phenomenon on my fish locator dial many times; and usually the result has been quick strings of good trout.

A third invaluable trolling trick is to mark the area where you experience a strike or where you see fish on your locator immediately, for the area is likely to be occupied by a number of trout. In a big open lake, it's almost impossible to judge the location of an exact point you troll through and then return to it. This problem can be licked by tossing overboard a small marker buoy the moment that a strike occurs or when you see a school of trout on your locator dial. These buoys are easily made by attaching a line to a piece of styrofoam, then attaching a sinker to the other end. When the buoy is tossed into the water the sinker will drop to the bottom, unwinding the line and holding the buoy in place.

A fourth key trick in successful trolling for summer trout is to use flashers or attractors ahead of the lure or bait. These chains

In the hot months, sharp trolling is usually the fastest and most effective way to locate trout in big deep lakes. Attractors or flashers ahead of lures increase the probability of strikes. (U.S. Bureau of Reclamation Photo.)

of flashy blades, keels and beads are deadly for summer trout in eastern as well as western lakes. Their use will increase strike frequency either when trolling for rainbows and browns, or when trolling for lake trout. The keels on good flashers will prevent line twist and proper flashers can help keep the trolled bait or lure at the desired depth. For example, the average three-foot flashers slow-trolled about thirty feet behind the boat on a fifteen pound test line will keep the lure or bait riding about eight feet under the surface. A four-foot flasher, fished in the same manner, will keep the bait riding about twelve feet under the surface. For deep trolling for lake trout a heavy drop sinker attached above the flasher is the most effective rig.

Lures and baits should be trolled about fifteen inches behind the flasher. Small and flashy wobbling plugs, such as the small silver or gold Flatfish, are consistently red-hot behind-flasher rainbow and brown producers. Small spinners, such as the small Hertig, the #1 Mepps and the 1/6 oz. Abu-Reflex, and small spoons, such as the Midget Dardevle, are also top rainbow and brown producers. Larger models of all the above lures are good behind-flasher lake trout producers.

Baits fished behind flashers will often take finicky summer trout when lures will not. The lowly worm fished behind a flasher is the undisputed bait king for summer rainbows and browns, while small strips of sucker meat, or similar forms of cutbait, are hot lake trout baits and will outfish any other trolled bait except fresh minnows.

When summer trout are observed surface feeding, another seldom-employed trolling trick is often successful. This unusual trick involves trolling an unweighted fly on a long line and at fairly fast speeds behind the boat. Almost any fly, but especially small streamers, can be deadly when fished in this manner, and at times when trout will not hit a conventionally offered fly or a trolled lure.

Best Deep Lake Casting And Still Fishing Systems

Once a trout concentration is located by the trolling, electronic search or test-fishing methods just discussed, casting or still fishing in that area can be highly effective. Any of the type lures recommended for trolling are also top deep lake casting lures. Of course, it is necessary to add a small split shot or two on the line ahead of the lighter lures to permit easy casting and to get them down to the desired depths.

One of the most successful tactics for taking hot-weather lakers is to use a 1/4 to 5/8 oz. white or yellow jig sweetened with a piece of sucker meat. The jig should be cast out, allowed to sink to the bottom, then retrieved with a series of very slow jerks.

This sweetened-jig fishing technique will often take sluggish summer lake trout when no other method will.

The hottest method for extracting hot-weather rainbows from southern impoundments, and from many western lakes as well, is still fishing by lantern light. According to Dick Roberts, owner of Dale Hollows' famous Cedar Hill Resort in Tennessee, far more hot-weather rainbows are creeled by this method in Dale Hollow than by all other angling methods—and most of the trout are taken on canned corn!

Super Systems For Shallow Mossy Lakes

Many lakes, especially those which are comparatively shallow, are choked with moss during the hot summer months. And a moss-choked lake is among the most difficult of all trout waters to fish. The electronic fish finder is of little value in such a lake, for reading the bottom or for locating fish, for it will not search through thick layers of moss. And conventional angling techniques, such as trolling or usual methods of casting flies, hardware or bait, are next to worthless in such lakes. A typical mossy trout lake not only has a "floor" of moss, but it also has ragged moss reefs or banks rising to the surface. Even its open waters are usually filled with floating patches of the green stuff. Successful angling in such a lake requires the use of angling tricks which will keep lures and baits out of the moss.

Beating The Moss With Flies And Baits Behind A Bubble

An unweighted fly or worm fished two or three feet behind a plastic bubble can be dropped into open pockets in the moss. This terminal rig can even be dragged over layers of moss lying a few inches under the lake surface. While only one angler at a time can work a flyrod effectively from a small boat, two anglers can heave bubbles and fly rigs on casting or spinning outifts from the same boat easily and effectively. Far more water can be covered by casting the bubble and fly rig than can be covered by conventional fly casting; and flies or worms can be presented to wary trout at greater ranges than is possible with the flyrod. These are important factors when fishing a clear and mossy lake.

Bubbles, of course, serve two functions. They provide casting weight and they help keep the fly or bait on top of the moss. Best bubbles are the transparent variety, and those which are no larger than necessary for casting weight. Colored bubbles or oversize bubbles tend to spook trout.

Many test-fishing expeditions on mossy mid-summer lakes substantiate that small flies, most often #10's to #14's, and nightcrawlers or large earthworms, are the most dependable producers behind a bubble. The small flies are probably best because most summer flying insects are small. As in any kind of trout fishing, it pays to try to match the kind of hatch which is on the water; but matching the size is far more important than matching the color or type of insect. Earthworms or nightcrawlers should be lively and hooked through a small portion of the head section on a #8 or #10 hook.

When fishing flies, the use of very small diameter lines and leaders is desirable, of course. On the other hand, most lunker trout dive into the moss, often threading the line through many yards of thick green stuff before emerging for their first explosive leaps. To land these strong heavyweights, the kind of trout most of us fish for, a heavier than usual line is required. If one wants a reasonable probability of making fish hit and of landing a lunker, he should compromise on a line and leader of six or eight pounds test. The use of such large lines and leaders will reduce the effectiveness of flies and even worms somewhat, but it will make the taming of that lunker possible when you finally hook him.

Beating The Moss With Midget Hardware

It is amazing how effectively midget hardware can be fished on top of the moss. Tiny spinners, such as the #1 Mepps Black Fury and the smallest Abu-Reflex or Rooster Tail, and tiny spoons, such as the Midget Dardevle and Sprite, are light enough to ride just under the surface if they are retrieved properly. It is also amazing how effective these small lures in drab colors are for lunker trout in most clear and mossy lakes. The frog-finish Midget Dardevle and the new black and gold #1 Mepps Black

Fury are probably the world's best lunker trout producers in such water.

When using midget hardware, the pay-off technique is to cast to pockets of open water or over or alongside moss beds which lie just under the lake surface—and to keep casts short. Long casts in a mossy lake are a waste of time because lures cannot be kept shallow enough or cast with sufficient accuracy. Best hardware retrieves in the mossy lake involve holding the rod tip high and "jerking" the lure in just fast enough to keep it under the lake surface.

Light fishing outfits and light lines are, of course, desirable for fishing featherweight hardware. Again, however, using a line of less than six or eight pounds test makes it almost impossible to land a lunker in a mossy lake. So, use the heavier lines and, if necessary for easy casting, add a tiny split shot about a foot above the lure. Swivels should not be used ahead of spinners or ahead of spoons with an eye ring. However, spoons without an eye ring will cut lines badly and a tiny snap swivel should be used with them.

Beating The Moss with Float-Up Baits

A very radical still-fishing tactic is often highly effective in the mossy mid-summer lake. This tactic can pay big dividends when it is too rough to fish safely from a boat or too windy to cast flies or hardware effectively from bank or boat. This tactic enables the angler to fish on top of underwater moss, not in it, and to keep his baits exactly where he wants them, regardless of wind and waves.

This unusual angling tactic will work with any type of casting or spinning equipment. It involves filling a plastic bubble completely with water and attaching the bubble to the end of the line; then tying two snelled hooks to the line at foot intervals above the bubble. The hook nearest the bubble is then baited with a worm or any other sinking bait. The other hook, however, is baited with a "float-up bait" of the buoyant marshmallow or cheesemallow variety.

This unusual still-fishing rig is easily cast long distances and will stay put regardless of wind or wave action. The bubble will

Rig for bottom fishing on top of moss. Note bubble filled with water which acts as weight and which rests lightly on top of bottom moss. Upper hook is baited with bouyant cheesemallow or marshmallow-type bait which floats well off bottom.

stay on top of underwater moss and not dig in the green stuff as a conventional sinker will. The float-up bait will float above the moss and at the same time will help keep the natural bait on top of the mossy bottom.

The effectiveness of this method of still fishing with float-up baits is almost uncanny in any lake with a mossy bottom. In such waters it will usually outfish any conventional still-fishing rig by a wide margin.

CHAPTER 9

Super Stream-Fishing Systems for Trout

DOING HOT-WEATHER business with stream trout is a popular and fascinating enterprise. Yet, its frustrations are often great and its profits meager. Why? In most cases, these businesses operate in the red because of easily avoidable mistakes—such as operating at marginal locations, doing business at the wrong hours, or failing to use modern equipment and procedures of optimum effectiveness. This chapter is designed to help anyone doing summer business with stream trout to avoid these basic mistakes—and to swell his net profits.

Where To Do Business on the Dog Days' Stream

During the hot months, most trout streams are low, clear and warm. Because of these factors, most trout will be concentrated in the deep pools or runs in the stream. The sharp angler will concentrate his angling efforts in or near these deep-water trout lairs and avoid fishing shallow stretches which are almost certain to be barren of catchable-size trout at this time of the year. Any deep pool or run in a good stream is likely to contain hot-weather trout; however, the best deep-water trout lairs have certain characteristics with which every serious trout angler should be intimately familiar.

The best trout pool or run has fast water churning in at its head. A churning headwaters saturates a deep pool or run with oxygen, which all trout crave when the water is warm. Lunker trout, in particular, will spend most of every midsummer day with their noses in the churning headwaters. Of course, big trout will make feeding excursions to other parts of a pool or run and even into adjacent shallows, but that oxygen-filled headwaters helps attract them to the pool in the first place and actually holds them during most of each mid-summer day.

The best trout pool or run has ample cover, such as caves under boulders, undercut banks or submerged tree roots. Trout require protective cover for both security and survival. During an environmental test in a Colorado trout stream, identical pools were constructed, except that one pool had good underwater cover and the other had none. The pools were constructed so that the rainbows, brooks and browns could move freely from one pool to the other. An equal number of trout were placed in both pools during mid-summer periods when the stream was low, clear and warm. All big trout and most small trout migrated to the pool with good cover within a day or two.

The best trout pool or run is one of limited accessibility. A trout pool that is difficult to get to is, of course, more likely to receive light fishing pressure and to have more trout in it than an easily accessible pool. Many anglers forget that accessibility is not merely a matter of the distance of a stream from populated areas. There are good pools and runs on many heavily-fished streams near urban areas which receive minimum fishing pressure simply because they are difficult to approach. Deep pools or runs, boxed in by steep banks or cliffs, or those bordered by thick brush without paths, or those which lie a considerable distance from parking areas, fall into this category. Several of my favorite mid-summer trout pools on Virginia's Passage Creek, on New Mexico's Rio Grande and on Colorado's Arkansas River are lightly fished simply because there's no convenient parking near them—and a well traveled road parallels each of these streams.

Yes, a crucial key to success on the mid-summer trout stream is to confine your angling efforts to pools and runs which are deep and, when possible, to those which are difficult to reach and which have fast churning headwaters and good cover.

Best Business Hours On The Hot-Weather Stream

During hot summer days, the proper timing of a trout trip is of overriding importance. Trout in all mid-summer streams, except those which are extremely high and cold, almost always feed with greatest gusto for a short period following the crack of dawn. This frenzied feeding period rarely lasts more than a couple of hours and invariably ends before shadows are gone and sunlight strikes the water. Thus, being an early riser is likely to pay high dividends when angling for mid-summer trout.

Many anglers tend to overlook the importance of crack-of-daylight trouting during the hot months. Perhaps this is because it's so easy to stay in the warm sack when considering the alternative at 3 or 4 a.m. Or, perhaps it's because more trout activity is usually visible during late afternoons when most insect hatches occur. Late afternoons are the next-best mid-summer angling periods on most streams, but the most trout and the biggest trout are likely to go to the angler who is fishing at daylight.

The test diary kept by a well-known angler during the summers of 1968 and 1969 substantiates the wisdom of being an early-bird trouter during the hot months. This diary records 30 day-long trout trips to Colorado's big heavily-fished Arkansas River on clear sunny days during the months of July and August. During each of these trips, this angler fished from the crack of dawn until dark with only short time-outs for rest and food.

During these 30 days he caught a total of 480 rainbows and browns, for a daily average of sixteen trout. Two hundred and sixty-three of these trout, or 55% of the total catch, were creeled during the first two hours of daylight! And nine of the eleven trout weighing more than three pounds which he took during this period were also creeled during these two early-morning hours! In other words, during these July and August trips, those first two hours of daylight were more productive than all other daylight hours combined.

Of course, there are exceptions to any fishing rule. Fine catches of mid-summer trout can often be made any time of the day, especially when cloudy skies prevail. Night fishing for big browns sometimes pays off, too, in hot weather. On any mid-summer stream, afternoon fishing can be almost as good as early morning fishing when insect hatches stir up the trout. And, in extremely cold and high streams, late afternoons are usually the best of all fishing periods.

Making A Large Profit With Small Flies

On most low and clear mid-summer streams, tiny flies are the most dependable producers. This is especially true when angling for rainbows, cutthroats, brooks and average-size browns. On many small mid-summer streams, even those with wild trout which have never seen an angler, it is almost impossible to take trout consistently with flies in size larger than #14's—and #20 midges are often optimum.

A couple of summers ago, the author's son, Doug, located an

On many small midsummer streams, even those with wild trout, it is almost impossible to take trout consistently with flies in sizes larger than #14's and #20 midges are often optimum. (Courtesy, U.S. Forest Service)

amazing stretch of water on a tiny wilderness stream in the Colorado Rockies. This stretch of stream was a series of small beaver ponds in a mile-long marshy clearing. It was well hidden in a thick forest of pine and spruce and was accessible only by a long hike from a dim jeep trail. Every miniature beaver pond in the meadow which was deep and which was fed by a trickle of white water harbored fifteen to twenty inch cutts and 'bows.

Doug fished for three days before he conceded that he couldn't take these big trout which had never seen a fly on conventional flies and a leader of reasonable strength. He began doing business with those big wild trout only when he switched to #20 midges and a 7X leader tippet.

Since this revealing experience, Doug has fished midges seriously in hundreds of small and clear mid-summer streams, and except in a very few cases they have outfished his conventional offerings. Of course, with a tiny fly the angler can expect to hook only about one out of every ten trout that strikes, and with a 7X leader tippet he can expect to land only a fraction of the big trout he hooks. But the fast action which midges will generate on most small mid-summer streams is reward enough.

Of course, when the water is high and roily, larger and more visible fly patterns usually are best even on the small mid-summer stream, and larger flies often are better any time of the year on the large streams. Finally, on any mid-summer stream, cannibalistic lunker browns will be taken most often on large minnow-imitation streamers.

Increasing Your Lunker-Profits With Spoons

Hardware is a top mid-summer angling choice for the man who has a passionate craving to catch a trophy trout. Far more water, both horizontally and vertically, can be covered with hardware on the end of a spinning or casting outfit than is possible with flies or bait. Hardware can be offered at maximum distances from the angler, where the probability of spooking lunkers is minimum. Cannibalistic hot-weather lunkers, especially browns, can be motivated to hit properly fished hardware. And when fishing hardware it is possible to use lines of sufficient strength to enjoy a reasonable chance of landing a trophy trout when you finally hook him.

Experience convinces me that three categories of hardware constitute today's hottest lure inventory for dog days' trout in any stream, large or small. The first category includes 1/6 to 1/4 oz. spoons or spoon-type lures, such as the Midget Dardevle, Super Duper and Swedish Pimple. The Dardevle and Super Duper are deadly in the smallest streams, but small stream casting with hardware requires the highest degree of casting proficiency. Pinpoint casting to small pools, often through or under overhanging brush, is an absolute requirement. Don't try small-stream hardware casting unless you're prepared to achieve this proficiency before leaving home. The faster-sinking Swedish Pimple, as well as the Dardevle and Super Duper, is often good in the deeper pools of larger streams. For mid-summer lunkers,

Cannibalistic big stream lunkers are especially vulnerable to spoons or spoon-type lures.

the best Dardevle colors are frog-finish or plain silver; the best Super Duper color is silver and red, and the best Swedish Pimple color is silver.

A slow deep and "jigging" retrieve is the big secret in fishing spoons successfully for mid-summer lunkers. Casts should be made upstream or within 45 degrees of upstream to the heads of pools. Then the spoon should be "jigged" or "jumped" slowly downstream and near the bottom. The retrieve is slow and deep enough only if the spoon can be felt occasionally bouncing along the bottom. The angler who doesn't occasionally hang up when fishing spoons is retrieving too fast and shallow to catch big trout.

Doing Hot-Weather Business With Spinners

The right spinner fished correctly is one of the most effective of all lures for dog days' trout. Three categories of spinners are the most reliable trout-getters on summer streams.

The first category is small dark spinners. These spinners most often work best when the summer trout stream is low and air-clear. Such spinners include the #1 Black Mepps; the Abu-Reflex with orange body and feather, and black blade; and the Rooster Tail with black body and feather, and silver blade.

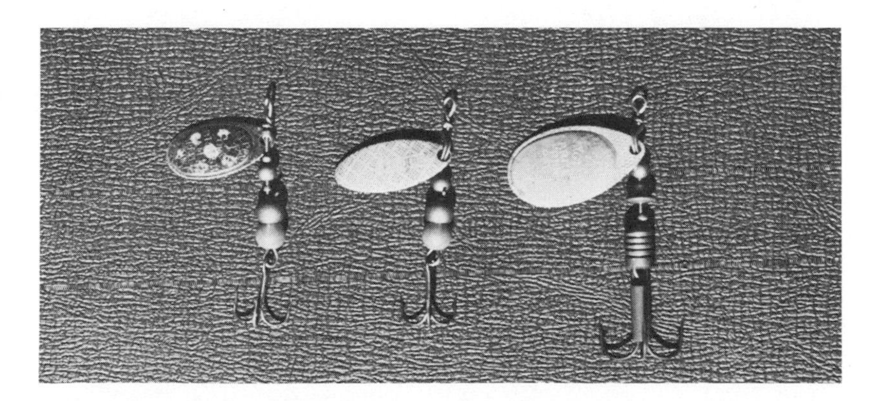

Small dark spinners usually work best when trout stream is low and clear (at left, #1 Mepps Black Fury). Small bright spinners are excellent when streams are slightly roiled (center, #1 Silver Mepps). Large bright spinners are best choices when stream is very roily or muddy (at right, #2 Silver Mepps).

The second category of hot-weather trout-producing spinners are small bright spinners. These spinners are sometimes red hot in clear streams, too, but they are most often deadly when a stream is slightly roily. Top spinners in this category include the 1/8 oz. Abu-Reflex with white body and feather, and chrome blade; the #1 Mepps in silver or gold; and the 1/8 oz. Rooster Tail with green body and feather, and silver blade.

The third category of hot-weather trout-producers is large bright spinners. These spinners are usually best when a summer stream is very roily or muddy—summer conditions which are infrequent but which may occur after a heavy rain or follow-

Large bright spinners are top lunker brown trout lures, especially when the stream is roily or muddy. When fishing very deep pools, it sometimes pays to add weight a foot above the spinner.

ing a big release of water from an impoundment dam. These spinners include the #2 or #3 silver or gold Mepps; and the 1/4 oz. Abu-Reflex with white body and feather, and chrome or gold blade.

When angling for summer trout, spinners should be cast upstream and retrieved with the same slow and deep retrieve recommended for spoons, except spinners should be retrieved at an even speed and not "jigged" or "bounced" in. The correct speed for the downstream spinner retrieve is, of course, determined by the speed of the current. This correct speed is best achieved by retrieving the spinner just fast enough to feel its blade turning. As in hot-weather spoon fishing, the spinner is being retrieved slowly and deep enough only if it can be felt occasionally bouncing along the bottom.

When fishing for big brook trout and rainbows, small pieces of earthworm or nightcrawlers attached to spinner hooks will often increase trout strikes in hot-weather streams. When water conditions are right for bright spinners, silver spinners will usually take the most rainbows and cutthroats and gold spinners will usually take the most browns and brooks. When fishing for fun in waters where only a single hook is legal, all spinners recommended are fairly effective even when two of their treble hooks are broken off with pliers, or when a single hook is substituted for the treble.

Doing Hot-Weather Business With Plugs

Small trout plugs are light and difficult to cast, especially if there's any wind. Yet they are sometimes highly effective against summer stream trout. Small wobbling floaters, such as Flatfish, the Rapala and the Rebel, and small sinking wobblers, such as the tiniest jointed Mirrolure, are deadly summer-trout takers under certain conditions.

When fishing a moss-choked stream, floating plugs can often be fished with great effectiveness when sinking hardware cannot be fished at all. A small frog-finish Flatfish, often is an unbeatable lure for such streams. By dropping these little floaters into the small open pockets over open pools and by giving them a few slow twitches, the angler often can stir up fantastic trout action, especially brown trout action.

Small Rebels and Rapalas in gold finish and fished in low clear beaver ponds, can give any angler good strings of hot-weather brooks and browns. The angler who has never fished these little floaters will be amazed at the savage manner hot-weather trout will charge these lures on the surface, sometimes when they are lying dead still between twitches. No angler should head for a summer stream when he doesn't know water conditions without carrying along some of these small floating plugs. They can save the day if he finds the water extremely low and mossy.

Small sinking plugs, such as the Mirrolure, and even the small floaters fished as sinkers behind a couple of split shot, are sometimes highly effective in big deep pools and runs, too, especially when one is angling for big stocked trout in eastern streams.

Lines And Terminal Rig Insurance

Even the lightest lures just recommended for summer trout can be fished easily and effectively with any good trout-action spinning or casting outfit. For easiest casting, 4 pound test lines are optimum; however, it is best to use lines of about eight pounds test in order to cut down on spinner losses in fast, rocky streams and to reduce the risk of killing big trout by impaling a lost spinner in their jaws. With a reasonable amount of practice, any angler can learn to toss these light lures far enough to catch trout, even when using an eight pound test line.

As previously indicated, small snap swivels must be used with spoons which do not have an eye ring for attaching the line. However, swivels are unnecessary when using spoons with eye rings and when using any good spinner or plug. Swivels should never be used unless absolutely necessary, for their use with small lures cuts down the frequency of strikes. Double clinch knots should be used to attach all lures recommended to the line. Lure hooks should be checked frequently to make sure that none are bent and that all are sharp. When stream casting, no weight should be used ahead of any of the sinking lures previously recommended.

Swelling Small-Stream Profits With Bait

Successful bait fishing for trout in hot-weather streams requires as thorough a knowledge of proper tackle and techniques as does heaving the artificials. The flyrod is the best basic weapon for fishing the small mid-summer stream. There are two effective methods for stalking and casting bait to small-stream trout. The first is wading upstream and casting to the deeper pools. Because of the trout's sharp eyesight, this kind of stalking should be done from a crouched position and a fairly long cast should be made.

The second method of getting bait to small-stream trout without spooking them is to use cover to make pool approaches from the bank. When brush prevents an upstream cast, a good pool can often be approached successfully from the bank by the resourceful angler. The trick is to use brush or a boulder for cover, to creep up on the pool, then to simply lower the bait into it.

The angler who strikes out using either of these two small-stream methods usually does so because he spooks his sharp-eyed quarry, either because his casts are too short or because he approaches the pool carelessly. Short leaders are essential for making reasonably long casts on the small brushy stream. And leader tippets should be kept down below four-pounds test when fishing baits in the small summer stream, especially when the water is air-clear and low.

Worms are the most dependable and easily obtainable baits for most small-stream fishing, especially for brooks and browns. Small to medium-size earthworms native to the area being fished are usually best and should be hooked on a #8 or #10 hook so that plenty of worm rear-end is left free to wiggle. Salmon eggs fished two to a #10 hook are usually best for rainbows and cutthroats in small mid-summer streams. Before using eggs, make sure they are legal in the waters you intend to fish. Soft red Fireball salmon eggs or canned corn are by far the best producers when angling for small-stream rainbows, but cutthroats usually prefer conventional white eggs. Worms, corn, and eggs produce best on the small stream when fished without weight or with only a tiny split shot ahead of them.

Doing Business With Bait On The Large Stream

The bait-fishing tactics just described, with the flyrod as the basic implement, will take trout on large mid-summer streams, too; however, other tactics and different baits fished with a casting or spinning outfit are generally superior on big summer streams. Only the spinning or casting rod provides the casting range required for the effective exploitation of most big streams. With these long-range rods, the angler can work his baits far ahead in deep pools, and even in mid-stream pools and in pools on the far side of the stream.

Easing upstream and making fairly long casts is usually the most effective method of bait fishing a hot-weather stream, especially when the water is clear. Big water generally means the presence of at least some big trout, the primary objective of most anglers. And the use of large natural baits usually provides the bait fisherman his highest probability of getting a hook into a tiger-toothed lunker. In most big streams, cannibalistic trout feed primarily on small chubs, suckers or other rough fish. Therefore, the type of rough-fish minnow native to the stream you're fishing almost always makes the superior lunker trout bait. Crayfish are also a top and often unappreciated mid-summer bait for trophy trout, as is a three or four inch strip of sucker meat.

Live minnows are best, of course, for big hot-weather trout, and they can be kept alive in easily carried bottles if the water is changed frequently. It is possible to take lunker trout, however, by using dead minnows which are salted down and frozen in small plastic bags; a handy point to remember if you fish waters where live bait is not legal. One of New Mexico's most proficient lunker-trout collectors fishes entirely with crayfish in the mid-summer months. He works big pools in the Rio Grande Box just below the Colorado border, and each year he takes several browns and rainbows in the five to ten pound category. Other pros on the Rio Grande and on Colorado's Arkansas River take mid-summer monsters with sucker meat strips.

When fishing for lunkers with any of the large baits just described, it makes good sense to use at least a ten pound test line. A # 4 or # 6 hook is generally best when using these large baits, and most old pros I know fish these baits on a #5-shot sinker rig. This rig consists of five small split shots clamped at inch intervals on the line with the first shot positioned about a foot above the hook. This rig tangles in rocks far less frequently than does a single larger sinker and it allows the bait to float more naturally with the current.

All these larger baits are usually more effective when cast upstream or across-stream to the heads of deep pools or runs. The bait should then be allowed to bounce along pool bottoms

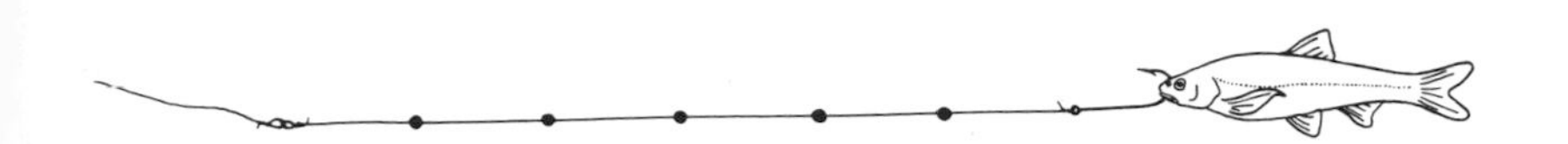

Five-shot sinker rig for fast-water trout. The rig minimizes snagging on bottom—allows bait to float more naturally with current.

with the current, with slight line tension being maintained by a slow steady retrieve. However, two alternative methods for fishing large, natural baits will also work well on occasions. The first is to float the bait downstream from a hidden spot at a pool's head. The other is to still-fish the bait in the pool bowels from the same position. Of course, worms and salmon eggs can also be fished effectively by using any of these three large-stream angling methods, and smaller baits should be used if your're fishing a large stream which contains only pan-size trout.

CHAPTER 10

Special Trout Tactics for Opening Day

ABOVE THE HISTORIC town of Front Royal, one of Virginia's top trout streams drops out of the pine-studded Blue Ridge Mountains to help quench the mighty thirst of the Shenandoah River. Passage Creek has all the intriguing characteristics of a fine trout stream; fast, cold, brush-lined headwaters; lazy runs meandering through meadows; churning, boulder-stewn rapids connecting deep, rocky pools. Some wild brooks and rainbows abound in the cold headwaters of Passage Creek, and the rest of the stream is heavily stocked with hefty brooks and rainbows just prior to the April opening of Virginia's trout season. Because of its proximity to Washington, D. C. and several other cities, Passage Creek is lined with hundreds of eager anglers on every Opening Day.

Most eastern streams are like Passage Creek on Opening Day: beautiful, trout-loaded, but crowded—so crowded that any angler who scores must have a special set of trout-catching tactics up his sleeve. This chapter is designed to arm the angler with these essential Opening Day tactics.

Licking The Opening Day Mental Jinx

One trait is always evident in any successful trout angler: a confident and positive attitude. Such an attitude is especially important, and too often lacking, when the average angler heads for the Opening Day trout stream knowing its banks will be lined with fishermen. Actually, there's usually ample reason for a confident and positive attitude on most Opening Day streams, even those most heavily fished. Most crowded trout streams, like Passage Creek, are heavily stocked just before Opening Day, usually with some very respectable trout. Most eastern states are now stocking brooks and rainbows as big and brawny as most wild trout in remote western streams. And anglers should forget all those ill-founded gripes they hear about "dumb and spunkless hatchery trout." When he's on the end of your flyrod or casting or spinning outfit, a trout is a trout, regardless of the manner in which he was raised. Most hatchery-raised trout fight just as well as most wild trout. And sometimes a big hatchery-raised trout is a lot harder to catch than a wild trout that has never seen a fly or a spinner.

Yes, it makes sense for any angler to head for his Opening Day trout stream knowing his opponents are probably numerous, of good size and worthy battlers. Then he'll enjoy fishing in spite of the crowds, and he might take a limit of good fish—provided he doesn't underestimate his quarry and try to score without preparing properly or by using sloppy angling tactics.

Choosing The Best Stream To Fish

In many states, opening trout season dates vary from stream to stream; and some streams, of course, are stocked more heavily than others. Therefore, a schedule of stockings and stream opening dates are valuable trip-planning aids, especially to anglers who plan to fish any area for the first time. These schedules can be obtained by dropping a note to game and fish agencies of states within the angler's radius of interest. It is good practice to select several streams which stocking schedules show to be heavily stocked, then to check out these streams, if possible, just before the season opens. This pre-season reconnaissance provides a basis for comparing the streams and the conditions of water in each, and for deciding on which stream to fish and where to fish it.

The final decision on which stream to fish will, of course, be influenced by fixed time and distance considerations such as the distance of various streams from the angler's residence and the relationship of stream opening dates to his free-time schedule. But other considerations are important, too. Choosing a stream which shows promise of being reasonably clear and ice-free will increase chances for a limit of Opening Day trout, for trout will strike more readily in such a stream. However, neither ice nor snow will stop the sharp angler willing to work from taking some respectable Opening Day trout, provided he is equipped with a vehicle capable of transporting him to the stream. Choosing a stream which is difficult to get to and which is located a reasonable distance away from larger cities in the area also will increase odds for creeling Opening Day trout, for the angling competition is likely to be lighter there. And the angler's detailed observations along various stretches of each stream, including the characteristics of specific trout pools, are highly important considerations in making a final decision on which Opening Day stream to fish. These considerations will be discussed in the next two sections.

Choosing The Best Stretch Of Stream

The most promising choice of a specific stretch of stream to fish is one with many deep pools, for this is the kind of water which the majority of early-season trout will hole up in.

On most heavily-stocked trout streams, a stretch of water with deep pools will probably be a good Opening Day fishing bet whether that stretch of water lies alongside a road or is remote from roads. A stretch of deep trout stream adjacent to a road is likely to be heavily stocked and will contain the heaviest concentration of trout when the season opens. On the other hand, after being stocked, some trout will quickly depart from that point of the stream and occupy deep stretches of water remote from roads. These remote stretches will contain a lighter concentration of trout, but opening-fishing pressure also is likely to be lighter there.

A predominately deep stretch of trout stream which is fed by warm water, such as exhaust water from a power plant or water emerging from beneath a deep-lake dam, usually provides excellent Opening Day fishing because cold-water trout tend to migrate to warm stretches of stream and to strike better in warmer water. And a stretch of stream immediately above a lake containing trout is always a promising Opening Day fishing choice. This is true because many early-season trout, especially rainbows, migrate from lakes up feeder streams to spawn and to feed.

Choosing A Good Trout Pool

During the recon trip it is also important to select a specific point on a specific pool to begin fishing when the Opening Day gun goes off. As previously indicated, the vast majority of trout in the early-season stream will be found in the deep pools, and the sharp angler who arrives early enough to claim a good casting position on a good deep pool, and who sticks with that pool using the right tactics, will often take his limit from it. Although covering a lot of water pays off when the crowds leave, it is not practical to move along a stream when it's necessary to fish through a long line of anglers.

The pool you elect to fish on Opening Day should be at least so deep you cannot see its bottom. Your odds for scoring will be even greater if the pool is also rippled by heavy headwaters churning into it, if it lies in a shaded area, and if it contains good trout cover, such as undercut banks, thick overhanging brush or submerged boulders. These factors cause trout to congregate in a pool and to strike better because they cannot see above-water activity or underwater lines and leaders clearly.

In addition to the characteristics just cited, the ideal trout pool to open the season on is one which can be fished only from a single casting position. Such a pool usually is too deep to wade and too brushy to fish from a bank, except from that one point which the sharp angler will homestead.

Also, there are many pools on most streams which can be effectively fished from several points, but most effectively from only a single position. A typical example is a large and very deep pool with a rocky point jutting out into it. By arriving early

A rocky point jutting out into a big deep pool is an ideal point to occupy on Opening Day.
(Courtesy, Tennessee Game & Fish Commission)

and claiming that point as his casting position, the angler can fish the pool effectively and havc ample casting room in spite of the presence of other anglers.

Opening Day Camping Considerations

During the preseason recon trip it is also important for the angler to note the location of the nearest campsite or parking area to the point he intends to begin fishing from on Opening Day, for his chances of claiming that point will be dim unless he arrives there early. A campsite or parking and camping spot immediately adjacent to an Opening Day fishing point is ideal. In addition to assuring a claim on a chosen Opening Day fishing point, camping out on a springtime trout stream is a totally invigorating and relaxing experience, and also the perfect time to dispose of that tough old vension or moose meat that is no longer greeted respectfully in the dining room. Even hatchery trout which are fried over a campfire and served to weary anglers always taste like manna from heaven. Best of all, eating the Opening Day's catch in camp provides excellent justification for fishing another day.

Super System Lures And Baits

Most Opening Day trout streams are likely to be higher than usual, colder than usual and more roily than usual. These probabilities usually give a big edge to the hardware or bait tosser over the flyfisherman. Nymphs and wet flies fished by an expert angler will take some Opening Day trout, but the average angler will do far better to leave his flies at home and to concentrate on using the right combinations of hardware and bait.

A small pocket-size hardware container will hold that lure assortment required on any crowded Opening Day stream. This assortment should include five or six of each of the following lures: # 1 Mepps spinners; # 1 Black Fury spinners; green and silver Rooster Tail spinners; Dardevle Midget spoons, in both silver and frog finish; and silver Dardevle Skeeter spoons. The tiny Skeeter spoons are easily fished on a flyrod. The other spoons and the spinners are too heavy to fish comfortably on a flyrod and are more effective when fished on the long-range spinning, spincasting or casting sticks.

To cast these lures effectively, a medium-size split shot should be attached to the line about six inches ahead of the Skeeter spoon and the Rooster Tail spinner. The other spoons and spinners can be cast effectively with no added weight, assuming the correct lines are used. It should be emphasized that these lures are recommended specifically for the typical crowded Opening Day stream where the quarry is average-size trout. When fishing for lunker trout in big, wild water, larger lures, as previously indicated, are often better.

Although the hardware assortment just recommended usually will get the angler who knows how to fish it a limit of Opening Day trout, baits can be effective, too. On any Opening Day stream, there's rarely any other bait as effective as salmon eggs for rainbows, and Fire Balls are the most effective of all salmon eggs. Early-season brooks and browns, on the other hand, usually turn up their noses at any kind of salmon eggs, but take worms consistently. And worms are usually fair rainbow baits for those waters where the use of salmon eggs is not legal. While cheese and marshmallow baits are top early-season baits for fishing lakes, they are rarely as effective for stream fishing as salmon eggs or worms.

Worms or salmon eggs can be fished effectively on either the flyrod or on any of the long-range casting outfits. Small, light-wire #12 hooks usually are best for fishing either of these baits on Opening Day streams. To get the bait down where Opening Day trout are, a small amount of weight usually is required about a foot above the hook on the flyrod leader which should be at least four feet long. And enough weight to hold the bait on the bottom should be added about the same distance above the hook when using the long-range casting outfits.

When fishing a crowded Opening Day pool, the angler will have little opportunity to maneuver around to unhook snagged hardware or bait hooks. If he tries to do so, he will usually interfere with angling efforts of others, or waste valuable casting time, or lose his casting point. Therefore, spinning or casting lines and flyrod leaders should be strong enough to enable the angler to spring the hooks of many snagged lures or bait rigs quickly with a sharp tug. When using the lures and hooks just recommended, eight or ten pound test monofilament is just strong enough to do this, and should be used.

Crowded-Stream Angling Systems

Thus far, the importance of choosing an advantageous casting point on a promising Opening Day stream has been stressed, as has the importance of arriving at that casting point early enough to claim it and with the right hardware and baits. The angler's Opening Day problem is now reduced to one of skimming the good trout out of that pool while other nearby anglers are fooling around. And the use of a few sharp angling tactics can make this remaining problem easy to solve.

First of all, remember that most trout in an Opening Day pool have never been hooked and have never seen a lure or bait, but remember also that this naivete will not last long once the Opening Day gun goes off and the lures and baits start flying. This means that the "iron will be the hottest" during that short period immediately following the season opening. And the sharp angler will strike while the iron is hot and with tactics specifically tailored to that situation.

Flashy lures cast upstream and retrieved downstream close to deep bottoms will be seen by the most trout, and will take the most trout in that "hot" period immediately following the season opening. Start off with those silver spinners or spoons previously recommended. Keep casts short and keep the lure traveling through the deepest water in the pool. Retrieve the lure fairly fast. This will take those trout in a hurry which are especially eager, and it will minimize snagging and resulting lost casting time during that critical "hot" period. This system of rapid fishing with flashy lures gives many sharp anglers their biggest Opening Day trout, and it often enables them to walk away with a limit of good fish before other anglers fishing the same pool get started on theirs.

Usually after thirty minutes or so of frenzied fishing pressure, the trout in any Opening Day pool begin to get lure shy, and as the day wears on and they are exposed to more and more angling pressure, they become increasingly difficult to catch. There are other tricks which the sharp angler can use to take good trout, even then.

Trick # 1 is to slow down the hardware retrieve! Finicky, lure-shy trout which won't take a fast moving lure will often suck in a spinner or spoon which is barely moving downstream and bouncing along a deep bottom.

Trick #2 is to change from flashy to drabber hardware. This is the time to start using those black, green and frog-finish spinners and spoons recommended earlier. Sometimes, finicky, lure-shy trout can be taken only on a drab and very slow-moving lure.

Trick #3 is to sweeten a spinner with a piece of worm. A #1 Black Fury Mepps with a half-inch piece of earthworm trailing behind one of the treble hooks will often produce the largest Opening Day brooks, and some good rainbows.

Trick # 4: If the preceding tricks fail, trail a small piece of worm on a # 12 hook on twelve inches of leader material behind a spinner. After an Opening Day pool has been heavily fished for a considerable perod of time, this combination sometimes works when no other hardware or hardware-bait combination will.

Switching to bait is often a highly productive tactic in a hard-hammered Opening Day pool, especially when the water is roily or muddy. Strong-smelling Fire Ball salmon eggs often work wonders on shy rainbows when fished dead still on a deep bottom. These eggs will soon be smelled by every rainbow in the pool and usually it isn't long before a 'bow begins nibbling them. These eggs are very soft and they will be sucked off the hook by the nibbling 'bows unless the hook is instantly set on that first twitch of the line. When fishing a hard-hammered Opening Day pool for brooks or browns, worms also work best when fished still on a deep bottom.

In pools with little current, a split shot positioned about a foot ahead of the hook will hold the bait on the bottom. If the current is strong and it is necessary to go to more weight to hold the bait still, it is best to use a slip sinker through which the line will slip when the trout mouths the bait. In order to free snagged hooks easily, it is best to start off with those eight or ten pound test lines or leaders previously recommended; however, if finicky trout refuse to take the bait, try switching to a lighter leader. There are occasions when even stocked trout in an Opening Day pool will take bait only when it's fished behind a fine leader.

Later on in the season when stream banks are crowd-free, moving along the stream and using those tactics described in previous chapters will take good carry-over trout. But on an Opening Day when the stream banks are lined with fishermen, the most fish will go to those anglers who use the special crowded-stream tactics just described.

CHAPTER 11

Super Systems for Winter Trout

THERE'S NO NEED FOR any trout angler to waste his winter weekends hovering around a fireplace and only dreaming of fishing. Instead, he should live! This is heading for a snow-fringed stream or frozen lake where he can tune in to winter trout!

New tactics and new equipment can make winter trout fishing more fun and more productive than ever. This chapter will cover this new look in winter trout angling and detail when, where and how to fish for cold-water rainbows, brooks and browns.

When And Where To Fish For Winter Trout

There are no trout waters where rainbows, browns or brooks cannot be taken during the cold months. At any given time, however, certain winter waters are likely to produce far better than others. The first key to successful winter trout angling is being able to identify these "best bet" waters. Of course, this choice must be made from waters legally open for winter trout angling. Fortunately, such waters are plentiful today in most trout states.

Should I fish a lake or a stream? Which lake or which stream is likely to be best? What time of the day is likely to be best? These are the first questions faced by winter trout anglers. Careful consideration of five basic factors will help answer them all.

First factor: In any area, certain lakes and streams are always the best trout producers. Those same lakes and streams which produce the most trout in the summer months usually are the best winter trout producers. The experienced trout angler will know these best trout-producing waters and will make his selection of winter angling destinations from them. The inexperienced angler should familiarize himself with these best trout-producing waters by huddling with an experienced angler, or by obtaining a list of top trout waters from his state game and fish agency.

Any stream or lake with a marginal trout population is a poor place to fish—winter or summer.

Second factor: In most trout country, lakes are poor winter trout fishing destinations until sometime in January. The angler heading for a trout lake in December is likely to encounter just enough ice to prevent casting from the bank, yet not enough ice for safe ice fishing. Therefore, before January, a stream with a good trout-producing reputation usually is the better choice.

Third factor: From sometime in January until the ice becomes too thin for safe fishing (usually in March or April), lakes are dependable trout fishing destinations in any kind of weather. As will be pointed out later, very frigid weather can make it impossible to fish a trout stream effectively; however, once safe ice has formed, a lake can be fished effectively and without undue discomfort in the foulest winter weather by the properly clothed and equipped angler.

Fourth factor: Snow conditions and weather are critical considerations when fishing the winter trout stream. The higher stretches of most trout streams are usually bordered and occasionally arched by deep snowdrifts throughout much of the winter. Even these stretches of stream will produce trout during warm spells when floating ice and snow does not prohibit fishing them. However, attempts to fish such stretches of stream should be avoided by all except experienced anglers who know how to negotiate deep snow country safely with four-wheel drive or snow vehicles.

The lower reaches of most trout streams can be easily fished during much of the winter. Deep snowdrifts are rarely an obstacle on these lower waters; in fact, during much of the winter, fishing these lower stretches of stream is as easy as in the summer. Important exceptions are those rare winter periods when deep snows hold along the lower stretches of stream, and extremely cold periods when floating ice makes even these lower waters impossible to fish. During these periods the angler's only choice, of course, is to head for a frozen lake.

Proper angling techniques should produce stream trout any time the water is not cold enough to form floating ice, even when

Once safe ice has formed, lakes are dependable trout producers in any kind of weather. Small jigs and spoons and salmon eggs are top choices for under-ice rainbows.

the stream is rimmed with solid ice. However, the warmer the water in a typical winter stream, the faster the fishing. Therefore, fishing is usually best on any winter trout stream after a few days of unseasonably warm weather. During such conditions, streams often are more promising fishing destinations than are lakes. The best time to fish the winter stream is during late afternoons following warm, sunshiny days, for the water is warmest then. The best spots to fish on the winter trout stream usually are shallow shelves bordering deep pools on warm, sunshiny afternoons . . . and the deep pools themselves during all other periods. Other trout-fishing hotspots on the winter stream are points where warm exhaust water from power plants or from beneath deep-lake dams enter the stream.

One of the best of all trout hotspots on the winter stream is a point where warm exhaust water from beneath a deep lake dam enters the stream.

Fifth factor: In extremely cold water, brooks are more active feeders than rainbows or browns. The water temperature in streams throughout the Colorado Rockies, for instance, holds at 33 to 34 degrees much of the winter. In this extremely cold water, the brooks in these waters feed with far more energy and frequency than do rainbows or browns. The same is true of trout in any extremely cold lake or stream.

Consideration of the factors just discussed should help any angler select promising trout fishing destinations during the winter months. Now let's move on to important considerations pertaining to winter trout tackle and angling tactics.

Super Tackle For Winter Trout

This discussion will begin with a recommendation of hottest winter baits and lures for rainbows, brooks and browns, for these best baits and lures influence the selection of all other tackle, which simply functions to present the baits and lures effectively. Best winter baits and lures for these three most popular trout are listed in the chart below.

HOTTEST WINTER TROUT BAITS AND LURES

(*Note:* These are listed in most frequent order of effectiveness. Be sure to use only baits which are legal in the area you intend to fish. The use of live minnows and salmon eggs for trout fishing is *not permitted* in some areas.)

BEST BAITS FOR RAINBOWS: (For streams or ice fishing)	Red "Balls-O-Fire" salmon eggs; soft white salmon eggs; canned corn kernels; tiny strips of sucker or chub meat; cheese baits . . . all fished on a # 10 or # 12 hook.
BEST LURES FOR RAINBOWS: (For streams)	1/8 to 1/4 oz. silver Mepps or Panther Martin spinners; 1/8 oz. Abu Reflex spinner with white body and feather, and chrome blade; 1/6 oz. brown Rooster Tail spinner; smallest Rebel, Rapala, or Flatfish plugs in silver.
BEST LURES FOR RAINBOWS: (For ice fishing)	Silver Dardevle Midget spoon; 1/16 oz. white Beetle crappie jig by Ward; 1/16 oz. white Doll Fly jig.

BEST BAIT FOR BROOKS AND BROWNS: (For stream or ice fishing)	Small live minnows; small salted minnows; worms, strips of sucker or chub meat . . . all fished on a # 8 or # 10 hook.
BEST LURES FOR BROOKS AND BROWNS: (For stream fishing)	1/4 oz. silver and red Super Duper; 1/8 to 1/4 oz. gold Mepps or Panther Martin spinners; 1/8 to 1/4 oz. Abu Reflex spinner with orange body and feather, and black blade; 1/8 to 1/4 oz. Rooster Tail spinner with green body and feather, and silver blade; smallest Rapala or Rebel plugs in gold.
BEST LURES FOR BROOKS AND BROWNS: (For ice fishing)	Gold Dardevle Midget spoon; 1/16 oz. yellow Beetle crappie jig; 1/16 oz. yellow Doll Fly jig.

The winter trout baits and lures just recommended does not include a listing of flies because baits and hardware will outproduce flies on any winter trout stream or lake. However, an expert flyfisherman can take winter trout on small wet flies and nymphs in most winter streams, and even on tiny dry flies in warmer trout waters which support significant winter fly hatches. These fly waters, however, are usually restricted to warm streams flowing from beneath high dams backing up deep-water lakes.

The flyrod is ideal for winter-fishing small streams with the baits just recommended; however, the longer-range spinning, spincasting or baitcasting outfits are usually best for fishing baits as well as hardware in the larger winter streams. The new high-test, small-diameter six or eight pound test leaders and lines, such as Bonnyl, Stren, or Blonde, are ideal for most winter stream fishing.

Since trout are sluggish in winter and since most of the time winter trout hold along the bottoms of deep pools, it is desirable to use a small split shot about six inches ahead of the bait when fishing with the flyrod as well as with the spinning, spincasting, or baitcasting outfits. Lures and baits should be tied directly to the line. The use of swivels to attach baits or lures to the line should always be avoided; for excess wire ahead of a lure or bait will spook winter trout and ruin the action of many lures.

When ice fishing for winter trout with any of the recommended baits or lures, short rods and open-faced spinning or baitcasting reels are best. Close-faced reels tend to ice up badly—and to remove the ice, close-faced reels must be taken apart. The use of fine leaders or lines and no weight are the secrets to successful under-ice fishing for trout. For under-ice fishing with bait, even the new improved leaders or lines should not exceed six pounds test, and even smaller leaders or lines will increase strikes. When jigging with spoons or jigs, leaders or lines should be kept down to about eight pounds test for best results. This requires that the under-ice angler also equip himself with a small gaff if he's to have much chance of landing that lunker brown or rainbow that may grab his lure or bait.

Super System For Winter Stream Fishing

The point has already been made that deep pools hold the big concentrations of stream trout during the winter; and that the only time many trout venture from these pools is during unseasonably warm spells when some will feed in nearby shallows. Therefore, the first key to successful winter stream fishing for trout is to concentrate all fishing efforts in, or in the immediate vicinity of, the deeper pools of the stream. Fishing long shallow stretches of stream during the winter months is a waste of time.

The second key to successful winter stream fishing for trout is to approach and fish the deep pools in such a manner that you cannot be seen by the trout in it. This may be an obvious point to experienced trout anglers; however, failure to recognize its importance probably is the biggest reason most winter trout anglers go home empty handed. Most winter streams are low and air-clear, and sharp-eyed trout can spot a careless angler a long way off. Being detected by his quarry eliminates any chance of success the angler might have even if he does everything else right.

There are two tactics the angler can use to keep from being spotted by his quarry. One is to work upstream making reasonably long casts. The other is to use bank cover to shield his approach and conceal his presence while fishing.

When using bait or hardware on one of the long-range spinning, spincasting or baitcasting outfits, the upstream approach

The first key to successful winter stream fishing is to concentrate fishing efforts in or near the deeper pools. The second key is to approach and fish these pools in such a manner that you cannot be seen by the trout in them.

combined with reasonably long casts usually pays the biggest dividends. Using this approach and fishing method, the angler is always out of sight of his quarry, he can cover all the likely water in a pool in a hurry, then proceed to the next. Using this angling method, he also covers far more water than does the still fisherman. And his bait or lure is always moving and moving naturally downstream with the current. This combination of favorable factors usually insures the maximum number of strikes in any given period. When fishing in this manner, hardware should be retrieved downstream, close to the bottom, and just a bit faster than the current. Baits, with that small split shot ahead of them, should be allowed to bounce slowly and naturally with the current along the bottom.

Still-fishing with bait can also be productive in the winter trout stream, with the flyrod as well as with the longer-range casting outfits. Best results usually come from sneaking up to each good pool, using a bush or boulder for cover, and dropping the weighted bait into the deepest section of the pool. Often, several sluggish winter trout can be taken from each good pool on a still bait; however, lifting the rod tip occasionally and "walking" the bait around the bottom will usually generate the most strikes. Of course, the angler must expect a "long, dry spell" after he exposes himself by netting each trout. But by patiently waiting out these spells, he may fill his creel after fishing only a couple of pools.

Super System For Ice Fishing

As previously pointed out, ice fishing for rainbows, brooks and browns can be easy, productive and comfortable regardless of weather—and from the time safe ice forms on a lake, usually in January, until the ice again becomes too thin for safe fishing, usually in March or April.

In most frozen lake country, the angler must expect sudden and extreme weather changes. Therefore, ample cold-weather clothing and shelter are also initial considerations of paramount importance. One can always take off a layer of clothing or fish outside his shelter if the fishing day turns out warm and balmy, as many do. So, it is wise to prepare for the other weather extreme. When heading for a frozen lake, it makes sense to wear a couple of pairs of thermal underwear, wool pants and shirt, and to carry along heavy windproof outer pants and a jacket with a warm hood. For a warm and suitable shelter, a lightweight folding ice fishing house with a plywood floor and tent top is hard to beat. This shelter not only provides the angler mobility, warmth and wind protection, but it also acts as a "dark room" from which to observe the reaction of trout to lures and baits.

This portable shelter and dark room for observing trout, plus a modern, easy-to-use and fast-cutting ice tool, such as the Fin-Bore, Jiffy Ice Drill or augur, constitute the best insurance for easy and productive ice fishing any man can buy. All these will be discussed in detail in the following chapter.

The angler should pull his ice house over a hole, drop down his lure or bait and watch the results. If no fish show up after a few minutes, he should move to a new area, cut a new hole and look for fish again. When he reaches an area where he sees trout, then he should begin fishing in earnest. Cutting two or three connecting holes makes it even easier to see the trout below. This super ice-fishing system is far superior to old systems of sitting out on the open ice blind-jigging, or of fishing from an immobile permanent shelter over fished-out water.

Watching the reaction of trout from a darkened portable ice house is a quick way to confirm the relative effectiveness of lures and baits. Earlier recommendations of best lures and baits for under-ice trout were based precisely upon such observations. Jigging small Dardevle Midget spoons is a deadly system for teasing rainbows, browns and brooks into striking. The most strikes will occur as the spoon flutters down; therefore, long widely-spaced jerks are best when using such spoons. The small jigs recommended, especially the new rubber-body Ward Beetle, are more effective when jigged with short, fast jerks. Baits are far more effective when allowed to sink using no weight. Trout often will take the baits as they sink toward the bottom; but occasionally, leaving a bait still on the bottom will produce the most trout.

The biggest limitation of fishing from a darkened ice house is that the angler's vision is restricted to a depth of about fifteen feet, even in very clear under-ice water. However, in most lakes there are plenty of rainbows, browns and brooks present in water of this depth. In fact, during many periods, usually early in the morning or late in the afternoon, many schools of big trout will be caught just under the ice.

CHAPTER 12

Special Tactics for Under-Ice Lake Trout

THIS CHAPTER REveals potent new tactics for taking the king of trout, the mighty mackinaw or lake trout, from ice-covered lakes. These tactics were uncovered during a long series of ice-fishing tests just completed by the author. Many of these tactics will amaze even the oldest ice-fishing pros. Serious study and use of them can skyrocket any angler's lunker lake trout take.

Ice Fishing Houses And Ice-Cutting Equipment

Before discussing those new and unique tactics which will take under-ice lake trout when nothing else will, more discussion on ice-fishing houses and ice-cutting equipment is in order. The first basic requirement for successful under-ice angling for lakers is a suitable ice house. As in fishing for smaller trout, such an ice house must be completely dark in order to permit the angler to see what goes on in the water below. Blind jigging on the open ice or from a shelter lighted by natural or artificial light is a decidedly inferior way to fish for lakers for two reasons.

First, under-ice lakers take a jigged lure so gently—and usually "on the drop"—and they spit the lure out so fast after feeling its unnatural hardness, that only a very small percentage of lakers which strike will be hooked by blind jigging. In fact, the angler who is blind jigging will not even be conscious of most lakers striking his lure.

Second, except in lightly-fished, laker-loaded waters of the Far North, the angler must jig a long time for every strike by a big laker. Without being able to watch the fascinating activity which takes place around a jigged lure in lake trout waters, it is exceedingly difficult for a winter fisherman to stay out on the ice and put in long and arduous periods of lure-jigging. On the other hand, when fishing from a properly-positioned and completely-darkened ice house, the angler will find it fascinating to watch the many monsters which pass under his fishing hole. By their reactions to his lure, whether or not they strike, and even by

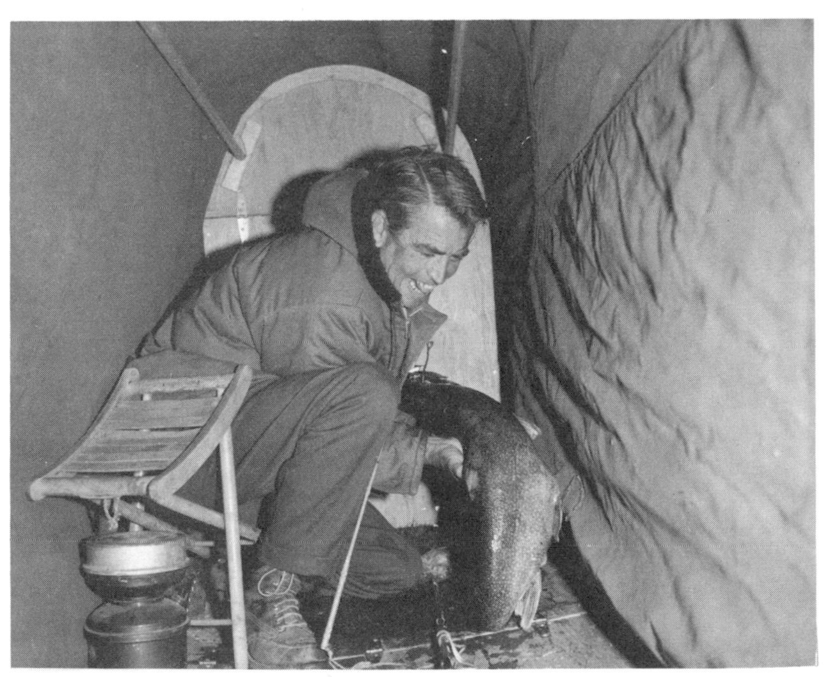

The portable ice shelter described in this and the preceding chapter weighs only 30 pounds, yet it is roomy enough for a small stool and heater.

watching the antics of smaller trout cruising near his lure, the winter angler will find that he can jig for hours and never become bored. Likewise, the angler who can actually watch big lake trout inhale his lure, will hook and land a far larger percentage.

The best ice house for under-ice lake trout fishing should also be portable.

As will be emphasized in this chapter, in a heavily fished area, lake trout quickly become "lure shy," even more so than smaller trout. After a period of sustained angling, the water below a permanent ice house becomes an inferior place to fish, even if the permanent ice house was located over a good fishing spot to begin with. Second it is usually necessary to fish many sections of a lake in order to locate the lakers' best feeding areas. For these two reasons, owning a portable, as well as completely darkened ice house is also a big key to successful fishing for under-ice lakers.

The most simple and austere, darkened, and portable ice house is simply a furniture crate, or other cardboard box large enough to accommodate an angler sitting on a small stool with enough space left to include the ice hole. Such a crude and inexpensive shelter permits some degree of observation in the water below, and under-ice lakers can be caught from it; however, such a shelter is not nearly as dark as a really good portable ice house; it wears out after a trip or two; and it is not nearly as warm and comfortable as a good portable shelter.

A first-class portable shelter has the following characteristics: a plywood floor (approximately eight feet long and four feet wide) hinged to fold into three sections, and with a fifteen inch trap door in one end which can be opened when the shelter is placed over the ice hole; two rounded plywood ends approximately four feet high (one with a door cut in it), attached to each end of the floor with hinges so as to fold down on the floor; a heavy canvas covering stapled to both the floor and the end pieces; two eight foot metal rods to be inserted inside the canvas and against the top side of the end pieces to hold up the end pieces and canvas. This kind of shelter weighs less than thirty pounds, It will fold into a small package, and can be easily transported or dragged across the ice by a vehicle or one man. It is easily erected by one man. And when erected, it is comfortable, windproof, and the only light which enters it comes up through the ice hole itself.

The requirement to move around in order to locate best under-ice laker feeding areas also requires efficient and fast ice-cutting equipment. Cutting a single hole through thirty inches of ice is a monumental task for any angler equipped with inefficient cutting equipment. Cutting several such holes with poor equipment in a single afternoon is almost impossible. Under-ice visibility for lake trout fishing requires a hole at least twelve inches in diameter, and preferably one of fifteen inches. Smaller holes do not enable one to watch a large jigged underwater lure or any of the fish activity around it. Also, a big laker is difficult to gaff through a smaller hole. But larger holes should not be cut as when abandoned, they constitute a hazard to other anglers through becoming concealed or obscured by the ice and snow forming over them.

Minimum equipment required for this kind of hole cutting is a highly efficient, non-mechanical ice drill, such as the Fin-Bore, with at least a seven-inch blade. When using this equipment, it is necessary to punch two, and preferably three or four adjoining holes to wind up with a single hole large enough to fish for lakers. A power drill, such as the Jiffy Ice Drill, will make the required hole-cutting task much easier and faster. A good power saw, with a long, wide-toothed ice-cutting blade, used in combination with either of the two drills recommended above, takes practically all the work out of frequent ice cutting. Since a car or snow buggy can be used in late winter on most frozen lakes with lake trout, use of the heavier-powered ice-cutting equipment then becomes feasible.

Any angler can confidently equip himself with a darkened ice house, plan to fish water five to fifteen feet deep, and know he will see lakers, including large ones—and know they will strike! This does not mean that the angler cannot catch an occasional laker by blind jigging in deep water. However, most fish caught by blind jigging in deep waters come from far northern lakes. While these, are reputed to be lousy with lake trout, most anglers just don't have the chance to fish this kind of water.

Owning a portable ice house which can be completely darkened and an efficient ice-cuttir tool such as the Fin-Bore, are the big secrets to successful fishing for under-ice trout. F directions on building the canvas and plywood house shown here, see accompanying text.

Tackle And Tactics

Larger lake trout feed most actively in the shallows during the early morning and late afternoon hours; and smaller lake trout feed actively in the shallows throughout the day. Far more lake trout in the over-ten-pound category will feed in the shallows during the early morning and late afternoon hours than during the mid-day hours. Smaller lake trout will remain in the shallows throughout the daylight hours. This means that the monster-hunter should be on the lake at daylight, rest during the middle of the day, and go back to his jigging in the late afternoon.

Best fishing spots for under-ice lakers are rocky shallows near abrupt drop-offs to deep water. The wise fisherman will punch holes in different spots until he locates a rock shelf ten to fifteen feet deep and dropping steeply down into deep water. Plain mud or sand bottoms or even rocky bottoms which slope down gradually to deep water rarely pay off. Rainbows, the principal diet of most lakers, are always more numerous along steep rocky bottoms adjacent to deep water. They hide in the rocks as lakers approach. The lakers probably feed in such areas because of the plentiful rainbows.

Under-ice lakers quickly become "lure shy" in heavily fished water. The angler usually will see as many big lakers jigging in a heavily-fished area as in a lightly-fished one. However, in lightly-fished water, a far greater percentage of lakers will strike his jig. This clearly indicates the disadvantage the angler imposes upon himself if he chooses to fish all winter from a permanent-type ice house. It also emphasizes the wisdom of punching holes away from the crowds, never fishing too long in one area, and of being equipped with that mobile ice house and those efficient ice-cutting tools previously recommended.

Very short rods and baitcasting reels with 20 pound-test monofilament lines are optimum for under-ice lakers. Jigging with the line (rather than the rod) held in the hand is most effective when trying to entice a lake trout into striking. After the fish is hooked, this requires a quick and smooth transition to the rod, a feat which simply cannot be accomplished with a long rod in the cramped quarters of a mobile ice house. Therefore, a very short rod is required for this kind of fishing. The rod should be no longer than three feet; it should have enough backbone to play a strong fish and yet be flexible enough to provide insurance against the line parting when attempting to hold a big fish close enough to the ice hole to gaff.

Good baitcasting reels, such as the Garcia Ambassadeur 5000, are far more dependable and easier to use when playing a big fish in cramped quarters than are closed or open-faced spinning reels. Big lakers are often lost by using a closed-face reel because the powerful runs of the heavy fish strip line off a half-filled spool too fast, breaking the line. Lines on open-faced reels tend to tangle during the transition from hand-held line to rod. All the problems are eliminated by switching to a good casting reel with its dependable star drag and visible line, all usable.

It usually takes at least two savage tugs to get a hook through the bony mouth of a big laker, and this job usually cannot be done properly with lines lighter than twenty-pounds-test.

Big Dardevle spoons, either silver or gold, and the same spoons tipped with sucker meat are the deadliest lures for under-ice lakers. The big Dardevle spoon configuration is probably superior to other lures because when it is jigged with a heavy swivel, it flutters rapidly, in a near horizontal position, and very slowly downward. An amazing number of strikes occur

Very short rods, baitcasting reels with 20 pound test monofiliment and big Dardevle spoons are an ideal tackle combination for under-ice lake trout.

during this slow, tantalizing downward flutter of the Dardevle. No other spoon flutters downward horizontally with as much action or as slowly.

Tipping the silver-and-gold Dardevles with sucker meat often increases laker strikes. To do this effectively, take the hooks off several Dardevles and re-attach them with a piece of wire so that the eye of the treble hook is dropped about an inch below each spoon. Then a frozen sucker, a needle, a spool of white thread and plenty of patience are required.

The rigging should begin the night before the fishing trip. A strip of meat for each spoon should be cut from a frozen sucker. Each strip should be about two inches long and taper from a width of about 1/2-inch at the top to a narrow "tail" at the bottom. Then each piece of sucker meat must be carefully sewed to each of the modified spoons. The broad "front" end of the meat strip should be sewed many times to the lower ring of the spoon and in such a way, that it dangles a fraction of an inch below the ring. Then the remaining meat strip which falls along the shank of the treble hook should be sewed to the shank. This leaves only a small portion of the meat strip dangling below the treble hook.

If sucker meat is sewed on each spoon in this manner, the meat will not tangle on the hooks; when jigged, the action of the meat is tantalizing, and each "sweetened" spoon will last for a long period. The hooks must be dropped down below the spoon, for most lakers will strike well down on the strip of meat. Failure to drop the hooks usually gives the striking laker only a bit of hookless meat. Finally, to keep the sucker meat on his spoons fresh and firm, the angler should refreeze the meat, spoons and all, before retiring.

Unusual techniques are required to hook and land under-ice lakers. When jigging, the angler's first problem is to attract big lakers. This is best done by covering as much water with the spoon as possible. This requires long upward jerks of the spoon with long pauses until the spoon flutters to the bottom. However, this same jigging action will rarely result in a strike after a big laker approaches and begins studying the lure.

The best system for actually teasing the lunker into striking, is to keep the spoon dancing in a small area with a series of fairly fast and even wrist jerks. The angler must learn to jig the spoon so that it never flutters out of his sight. If the lunker is going to strike he will usually suck in the lure on a downward flutter during these short and even up-and-down gyrations of the spoon. Frequently, big lunkers will make a dozen or more passes at the lure before they inhale it. During this wildly exciting period, it is difficult to keep from making a noise, but this is important, for any banging vibration against the ice house floor will cause the quarry to streak out of sight.

The second critical moment is when the lunker inhales the spoon or grabs the sucker meat dangling from it. If the angler does not strike at this very instant, the lunker will spit out the lure and leave the area. If the laker weighs over ten pounds, it is exceedingly difficult to get the hook through its bony mouth. Therefore, the angler must strike him with much force, and if the big laker's mouth is closed around the spoon on this initial strike, it is almost impossible to set the hook. So, the best practice is to set the hook hard two or three times in rapid succession. This action gives the angler a high probability of slamming the hook completely home at that critical and necessary moment when the big laker's mouth is open.

The angler's next problem is an exasperating one. When line pressure is applied to a big under-ice laker, instead of opposing the pressure, usually he will come right up to the hole as the angler pulls. Many do just this, and it appears that they are trying to overtake a fish they think is trying to escape them. However, when most hooked lakers reach the vicinity of the ice hole, they detect danger and all hell breaks loose! At this moment, the angler must control himself and make a smooth and effective transition from the hand-held line, now burning through his fingers, to his rod. If the laker gets slack line during this transition and is not firmly hooked, he will spit out the lure; and if the angler holds too taut a line during this transition even a twenty pound test line will part.

Once a successful transition has been made from the hand-held line to the rod, the angler should have his prize—provided he remains calm and patient enough to play his quarry carefully and skillfully. The biggest hazard during such battles, is the temptation to tighten down too much and too soon on the drag. When the angler sees a tiring laker of monstrous proportions right beneath his ice hole, it is difficult not to clamp down on the drag and attempt to gaff the fish prematurely.

A good gaff is essential for landing most big lakers through a hole in thick ice. Even if the angler tires his quarry down completely, it is almost impossible to drag a giant laker up into the ice hole, and a man's arms are not long enough to reach down below the ice and do the job easily. The gaff should have a handle about three feet long and the hook should have about a three inch curve. If commercial gaff hooks of this type are not available locally, any angler can make his own from a piece of quarter-inch steel rod and an old broom handle.

The tactics just discussed may seem radical. They are . . . but they work wonders on giant lakers when all other methods fail.

CHAPTER 13

Electronic Fishing Methods

THE ADVENT OF ELECTRONIC fish finders and electronic thermometers permits locating fish and promising underwater fish cover in a scientific, fast and effective manner. Preceding chapters mention the use of these modern angling aids. This chapter will discuss their use in more detail. As preceding chapters indicate, the value of any fish locator is greatest in deep lakes and rivers. This discussion will center around fishing this kind of water with these modern aids. It is presented through the courtesy of Lawrence Electronics.

How The Electronic Fish LO-K-TOR Works

The instrument's transducer sends a high-frequency sound wave (inaudible to fish as well as humans) through the water. When the echo returns, the transducer picks it up and converts it back into electrical energy. The unit times the interval and flashes a red signal on the dial. Since the dial is calibrated in feet, the signal shows the distance between the transducer and the obstacle that returned the echo.

Electronic fishing requires the use of two instruments: a fish locator and a thermometer which will read water temperatures at any depth.

What The Electronic Fish LO-K-TOR Tells You

The primary purpose of the instrument is to find fish. It does this for biologists studying fish as well as for anglers catching them. In addition, it has many other uses.

Since it tells depth accurately, it can be used for making contour maps of lakes, bays, inlets, or large streams, and for contour trolling over bottoms of desired depths. It is useful in navigation because it warns you when you are approaching shallow water. It will find the deep holes in large streams. It is useful in salvage operations because it will accurately show a sunken boat lying on the bottom. It even tells what kind of bottom your boat is passing over. It works through ice as well as water; therefore it can be used as an ice-fishing aid as well as for boat fishing.

Surveying A Lake

The most efficient and least time-consuming way to become acquainted with any body of water, no matter what kind of fish you are after, is to survey it with such an instrument. Start out with a map of the lake if possible; if you can't obtain a map, make sketches as you go along, indicating the promising spots in relation to landmarks on shore—and remember, it takes two landmarks lined up on one shore to establish a line across the water. It takes four landmarks, preferably establishing lines at right angles to each other, to pinpoint a specific spot.

As you go about your survey, the fish locator will tell you the depth and kind of bottom. It will also reveal, perhaps, schools of crappies or white bass suspended over deep water; possibly

How the FISH LO-K-TOR works: The LO-K-TOR both sends and receives signals. Received signals are indicated on dial. Red signal at "O" indicates unit is on. Red signal at bottom indicates bottom depth. Any signal between would indicate fish and their depth. (Lowrance Drawing)

Using FISH LO-K-TOR on ice: When using LO-K-TOR on ice, the transducer is placed in small puddle of antifreeze and water. (Lowrance Drawing)

bass or walleyes close to a gravel bottom at a depth of 20 feet or so. From experience, it doesn't pay to stop for single or widely-scattered fish. If rapidly repeated and multiple signals on the dial indicate a good school, however, it is worthwhile to stop and fish for them. You may not get any farther!

You should do your surveying at a fairly rapid speed. Have a piece of styrofoam, about the size and shape of a brick, with 50 to 100 feet of grocery string wound around it and a three-ounce sinker on the end, ready to toss overboard. When the instrument indicates a school of fish, throw this buoy out. The string will unwind until the sinker hits bottom. Then, because of the marker's flat shape, it won't unwind any farther to drift away with the wind. With the school thus marked, you can make your turn and come back to fish in exactly the right spot.

This is essential when you're far from shore on a big lake,

for unless you mark the school of fish when you're over it, you may not be able to find it again. Once the buoy is on the water, you can easily check the size of the school by making a couple of passes across it.

Using A Thermometer

Another tremendous help in discovering where to fish for any particular species is an electronic thermometer which will give an instant reading of the water temperature from the surface down to a depth of 100 feet as the probe is lowered. This instrument is second in usefulness only to the electronic fish locator. The latter tells where the fish are; the thermometer tells you why. It also gives you a good clue as to the species because different kinds of fish prefer different water temperatures. In the meantime, here is how Carl Lowrance and I use a thermometer to help find fish, even in lakes we fish regularly:

Suppose we're after largemouth bass. Immediately after launching the boat, we put our fish locator into operation and run offshore until we're over water about 40 feet deep. We then stop, anchor the boat if the wind is blowing, and lower the probe of the thermometer. If it shows 75 degrees at 20 feet and 68 degrees at 25, we know the bass will be between 20 and 25 feet deep because this is the temperature range they prefer.

Then, with the aid of the fish locator again, we limit our fish hunting to water of this depth, over the kind of bottom bass like. We contour rocky points, bars and reefs; follow drop-offs, and cruise across gravel flats until the instrument finds fish. Although it would find them eventually, anyway, the thermometer narrows down the search by enabling us to stay off water that is either too shallow or too deep.

Hunting Fish

While making the initial survey of a lake, you will naturally be looking for fish, too, and—as we mentioned—you may find them and never get any farther! In case you find only scattered individuals or small schools, however, here are some ideas:

Deep Water: Survey the deepest water in the lake with the fish locator. Work back and forth over the channel, whether it is 30 or 200 feet deep. For some reason—possibly because it is a

TEMPERATURES PREFERRED BY FISH

(Courtesy—Lowrance Electronics.)

SPECIES	PREFERRED TEMP. RANGE
Bass—Largemouth	68-74
Smallmouth	65-70
White	70-75
Crappies, bluegills, sunfish	68-78
Muskellunge	60-70
Northern Pike	50-70
Pickerel	50-70
Walleye	55-70
Perch—Yellow	55-70
White	65-70
Trout—Lake	45-55
Brook	55-65
Brown	55-70
Rainbow	60-70
Catfish—Channel	70-75

little cooler or there is a current—bait fish often prefer to feed over the channel in the deepest area of the lake, even though they stay within five feet of the surface.

When the quick, light flashes near the surface indicate bait fish on the instrument's dial, search the area carefully. Most game fish follow their food supply. The dial may well reveal game fish directly below the school of bait fish or else somewhere nearby.

Bait Fish: The importance of bait fish to successful fishing can't possibly be over-emphasized. They are the principal food of all game fish in most waters. When you find them, the big fellows usually aren't far away. (By bait fish, incidentally, we mean the plankton-feeding forage fish, such as threadfin shad and gizzard shad, minnows, young rough fish such as carp, and also the young of such game fish as crappies, bluegills, and white bass, which also feed near the surface.)

Most bait fish are concentrated within five feet of the surface where sunlight promotes the growth of the plankton on which they feed. We usually hunt the bait fish first. When we find them, we know the game fish probably will be somewhere nearby—

often directly beneath the school of bait fish and between 12 and 25 feet deep.

It is when these game fish come up to feed, of course, that we see the exciting disturbances on the surface—boils, swirls, splashes, minnows flying into the air, and birds swooping at them from above. When this occurs, we don't need the fish locator. But with its help we can often catch fish when they're not feeding on the surface because we can put our lures down where they are.

Fish The Windward Shore

Years ago, the guides in Maine and Canada taught Carl to fish near shore on the windward side of the lake when the whitecaps started rolling. They said the walleyes and bass were catching minnows injured by the waves and rocks. The guides were only partly correct. The bass and walleyes were there feeding on minnows, all right—incidentally, trout and many other game fish feed here, too—but few, if any, of the minnows were injured. They had simply followed the drifting plankton on which they feed. And since the minnows had followed their food, the game fish followed theirs.

Shortly after a steady wind comes up, the plankton will start drifting. We have found that by working from mid-lake toward the windward shore with the fish locator we often find bait fish following the plankton—and game fish following the minnows. Then, after the wind has been blowing for awhile, we look for a windy point, reef, or shore with the waves rolling in and deep water—20 feet or more—within casting distance upwind.

We cruise back and forth, prospecting this water with the instrument. As soon as we find the fish, we beach the boat in a safe spot and walk back along the shore to an area where the fish are. Then, using weighted plugs, jigs, spoons, or spinners, we cast into the wind. This is important! The game fish are facing into the waves and moving back and forth parallel to the shore in search of food. By retrieving with the wind, we bring our lures toward them from in front, the same direction from which their natural food is approaching. This method is far more effective than staying off-shore in the boat and retrieving so the lures approach the feeding fish from behind.

We have also learned to fish the deep coves in summer and fall when the wind has been blowing into them for two or three days. Then these coves are often full of bait fish—with hundreds of crappies, white bass or other game fish nearby.

If the wind changes, however, and blows out of the coves for several hours, the fish usually go to another area. It is really surprising how a cove can be fairly stiff with fish one day, yet have none at all the next.

Fishing The Right Depth

After the electronic fish locator finds the fish and tells how deep they are, you still are faced with the problem of keeping the lure at the proper level. Many times, fishing only a foot or two below or above the correct depth catches nothing, while working the lure exactly at the level of the fish would bring a strike on every cast. There are a number of tricks that help in this respect.

Marking Line

A color-coded, lead-core trolling line is fine when used in the kind of fishing for which it is adapted. With a different color every ten yards, you can keep letting out line until you catch a fish; then, by letting out the same length again, continue working your lure at the same depth so long as you maintain the same speed.

You will soon discover, however, that for many kinds of fishing a lead-core line simply isn't suitable. Nor does the color change every 30 feet provide the precise control necessary for best results. Carl and I have found that marking our regular monofilament lines at five-foot intervals is well worthwhile, and the method we use is quick and easy.

First, we dissolve a package of black household dye, Rit or Tintex, in a gallon of water, using an enameled container. We then wind the line endwise around a light board six inches wide and five feet long. We heat the dye—but don't boil it—submerge one end of the board, and let bucket and board stand in the corner for 20 minutes. We inspect the dye job by rinsing off the surplus under cold running water. If it is satisfactory, we repeat the process with the other end of the board.

We sometimes dye four or five lines of different tests at the same time, fastening the ends of each to the board with an ordinary office stapler. We attach the board at the middle of one edge to the corner of a table with a C-clamp while winding the line on and off. And by doing both from the same side of the board, we avoid twists. The dye, stored in a glass jug after each use, keeps indefinitely.

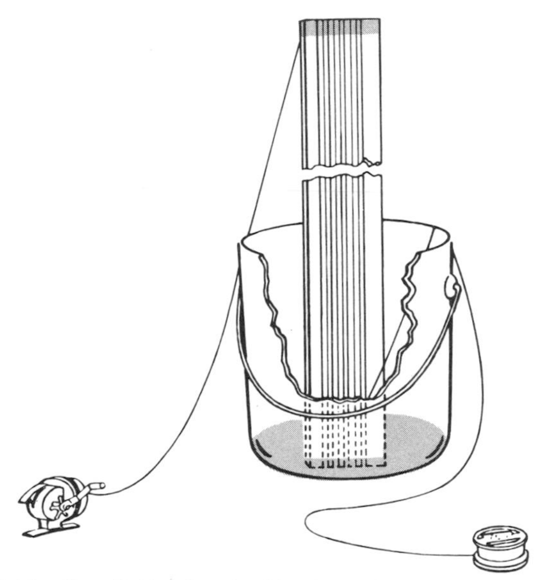

How to dye fishing line: Fishing line dyed in alternating five-foot sections aids fishing depth control. (Lowrance Drawing)

Using The Marked Line

We have found line marked at five-foot intervals to be useful so often, for so many different kinds of fish the year round, that we habitually dye each new line when we bring it home. In the summer, we drift or troll slowly across schools of suspended fish and count the marks as they run out through the guides until we catch one. If six marks had gone out, meaning trolling 30 feet of line, we can continue to fish at this depth so long as we maintain a constant speed.

A word of warning is necessary here: With monofilament line and any given lure, or a sinker of any given weight, you can only fish so deep. Contrary to the old bromide, your lure won't work deeper and deeper as you let out more line beyond a certain point. Instead, the line forms a parabolic curve within and under the water, and trolling 50 yards of line may not get the lure one inch deeper than trolling 50 feet. Skin friction of water on the line will put more resistance on the line and have a tendency to straighten the line, thus causing the bait to run more shallow. This is especially true with non-metallic lines, such as monofilament.

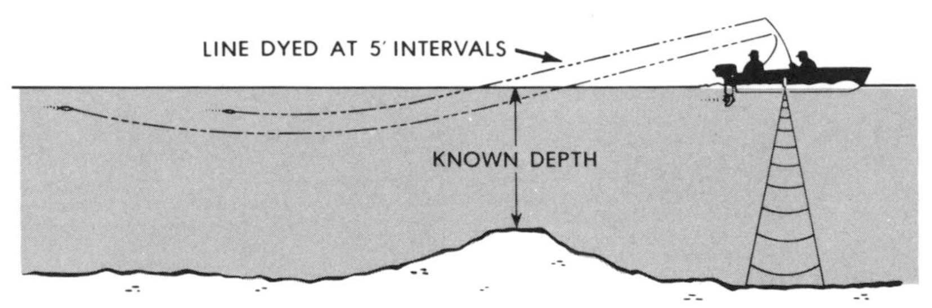

Trolling with long line: Letting out more line may not increase lure depth, due to line friction and trolling speed. (Lowrance Drawing)

The simplest way to determine how deep various lures run is to troll them over a clean gravel bottom at known depths, maintaining a constant speed and length of line. This is easy to do with the electronic fish locator and marked line. If a lure bumps bottom steadily at a depth of 10 feet, but not at 15, you can be sure it will be right among fish suspended at 12 feet over deep water, provided you troll at the same speed and use the same length of line. Mark lures so tested with lacquer or fingernail polish. Three figures will do it—for example 12-40-3—meaning the lure runs 12 feet deep on 40 feet of line at a speed of three miles per hour.

Being able to control your speed accurately is the key to successful trolling, but doing so is far from easy when you may be alternately heading into the wind and then running with it as you move back and forth above a school of fish.

You can use your marked line as a guide. Let your lure sink to the bottom in shallow water, then head the boat away from it and count the dyed spots as they run out through the guides. This table shows the number of dyed spots, five feet apart, that run out at speeds from one to six miles per hour during a 10-second interval.

Marks	Speed
3	1 mph
6	2 mph
9	3 mph
12	4 mph
15	5 mph
18	6 mph

Actually, knowing the exact speed is not so important as being able to maintain a uniform speed. You can do this by timing the marked spots as they run out. Obviously, this rough-and-ready method would never do for timing races. But when you're trolling back and forth across a school of fish, it's far more accurate than watching a distant landmark on the shore.

Contour Trolling

Bottom bumping is a simple and effective method of catching bass, walleyes and other fish that spend a good share of their time hugging the bottom at various depths between 10 and 30 feet. Determine with your thermometer or by starting at ten feet and fishing deeper and deeper until you connect, the depth they prefer at that particular time. Then, with the aid of the fish locator concentrate on clean gravel, sand, or rocky bottoms at that depth. You can do this by contouring points, working back and forth across long, sloping bars—sometimes 100 yards from shore—circling islands, and following submerged reefs. Troll, of course, with a bottom-bumping lure.

This is essentially what scientific electronic fishing is all about. Its principles can be used in many ways and in conjunction with most fishing systems previously discussed.